Ban Those Bird Units!

15 Models for Teaching and Learning in Information-Rich and Technology-Rich Environments

David V. Loertscher

Carol Koechlin

Sandi Zwaan

Hi Willow Research & Publishing

Hi Willow Research and Publishing
312 South 1000 East
Salt Lake City UT 84102

Distributed by:
LMC Source
P.O. Box 131266
Spring TX 77393
800-873-3043
sales@lmcsource.com

ISBN: 1-933170-11-5

In Appreciation

We express appreciation to the many colleagues and students throughout the years who have helped shape and test the ideas in this book. Graduate students at San Jose State University have been particularly helpful in their input, particularly Tahana Lish and Patti Stein who read the final manuscript carefully and supplied many suggestions.

Contents:

List of Sample Units

List of Sample Units by Discipline and Grade Level

Fine Arts

Introduction for Teachers

There are certain types of research assignments that contribute little or nothing to learning. Teachers should recognize such low-level activities and re-design to build achievement

What is a "bird" unit?

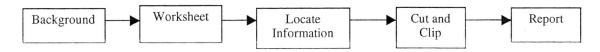

A bird unit usually follows this common pattern:
1. The teacher provides background to a topic in the classroom (could be birds, presidents, countries, states, people, etc.).
2. Textbook work is done.
3. The teacher asks the class to do a project in the library or computer lab and provides a worksheet for data collection. The worksheet contains fact questions.
4. Students pick a "bird" to research and go to the library or computer lab where the librarian or technology coordinator introduces them to a few resources.
5. Students copy information from information sources onto their papers.
6. Students report back to the class or turn the papers in for a grade.

Why is a "bird" unit generally a disaster?

When the majority of research in the library or computer lab is merely the cutting and clipping of information into some sort of report, little learning takes place. In the age of technology, students can easily cut and paste megabytes of information from the Internet or electronic sources and turn them in as a report. Obviously, time in the library or computer lab is underused and little progress toward educational achievement is made. In fact, assignments like these encourage plagiarism.

What is to be done?

1. Re-design the activities so learners must THINK ABOUT and analyze the information they collect in the library media center, thus increasing learning and achievement.

2. Re-design activities so that learners must DO SOMETHING (synthesize) with the information they collect (such as sense-making, performing, trying out, acting, building, etc).

3. Keep redesigning activities until number one and number two happen.

This book contains fifteen models to use, as the classroom and the library and/or computer laboratory are merged for a learning experience. Each model is designed to insure that students develop understanding and build knowledge. The design of each model requires students to not just cut and clip or extract information, but forces them to use that information in a higher-level thinking activity. The objective of the Model is preparing students to achieve and learn more in the real world of information and technology. The models do not ask you to abandon any successful teaching method, but suggest simple changes to elevate the learning experience dramatically. The models are based on experience and educational research and are designed to work in an information-rich environment pictured below.

Reflecting on transformed learning experiences:

As the collaborative team plans, transforms, or reinvents a learning experience into one of the models of the book, here are some reflective rubric-like statements to consider. The transformed unit:
1. Was true to the model or was a creative adaptation of it.
2. Caused students to use higher-level thinking resulting in deeper understanding. We are confident that the students learned more because of our new design.
3. Made use of QUALITY information resources and APPROPRIATE technology.
4. Integrated information literacy and technology skills into the learning experience.
5. Was a true collaboration of teachers, librarians, and technology professionals.
6. Was so successful that we plan to do it again, or we know how to tweak it to make it even better next time.

How to Use This Book

Each of the 15 sections is structured as a quick guide for using the model presented as a planning guide or a guide for professional development using the following features:

1. The **model** itself providing an explanation in words at the top followed by a diagram of the model. This is followed by reasons why this model is an effective approach, sample topics that work well with the model, and critical information literacy skills with links to the companion volume by Koechlin and Zwaan,

2. Each model is followed by a brief, two-page description of the model in more depth and giving suggestions for its use. All **notes** sections end with a section on technology, giving suggestions for integrating tools or software into the model activity.

3. The notes section is followed by a page describing **critical information literacy skills** students will need to handle the information or data they will encounter when they use the model. Each of these critical information literacy skills and others that might be appropriate are amplified in the companion volume *Build Your Own Information Literate School* published by Hi Willow in 2003.

4. Two **brief examples** of learning experiences follow the model. Since each model can be used from K–12 and across all disciplines, the brief examples are varied in their topics and grade levels. Worksheets to be used with the examples are after the examples.

5. One or more **longer examples** follow. These include tips for identifying evidence of student understanding and prompts for teacher reflection to customize the experience and insure student success. The topics vary across the disciplines and grade levels and provide more detail as idea starters for teachers. Useful worksheets, if needed, are provided after each example.

The final section of the book contains popular educational models from numerous authors that work well in information-rich environments. On each page, the popular model has been reproduced or charted together with suggestions on how to tweak those models when information resources are plentiful.

Introduction for Educational Leaders

Why such a crazy Title? What are Bird Units? And why do you have something against birds?

For decades, school, public, and academic libraries have been plagued by "bird units." Bird units come in two different species: Fill-in-the-Blank Worksheet Birds, and Report/Term Paper Birds. So ubiquitous are these two species that they have crowded out every other kind of beneficial species and are as welcome as a New York City pigeon or a crow in a garden patch.

Permit us to illustrate.

Story One:

Teacher X is faced with teaching the "bird unit" for the tenth time in a decade of teaching. The bird unit topic could be Civil War, California Missions, old/famous/white dead men…etc., ad infinitum. The unit is to last from Monday until Friday. Days one and two are taken up with a brief introductory lecture, the reading of a textbook chapter, and having students answer the chapter questions.

Wednesday. Time for a change of pace. Search the files. Find that sheet with all the purple writing on it (you have to be old to understand this joke). Take the worksheet to the copier and now you have a worksheet printed in black. Breeze past the library to inform the librarian of the impending invasion.

March the class to the library. Give each student a worksheet. Say: "Pick a bird—any bird and answer the questions." Hopefully, the librarian has had time to pull the bird books onto a cart for easy location. Students rifle through the books looking for "their bird" and the answers to their questions.

To young Susan's dismay, there isn't a whole book on the Rocky Mountain spotted woodpecker. She grumbles, adding to her tally that once again this library is a failure. Juan is disappointed because he did find a book on the ruby-throated hummingbird, but the answer to the first question was not on the first page, so he bops Susan on the head with the book and they both start fighting. Since teacher X has escaped the scene to the teacher's lounge, the librarian calms the troops and helps everyone find something to use.

The worksheet assignment is to locate a few facts, and we know them already:

What does my bird eat?
What color is my bird?
Where does my bird live?
Does this bird migrate? If yes, where?
Etc.

Forty-five minutes later, the teacher re-appears, gathers the chicks, and for the next two days, students do reports in the classroom on their birds.

The last activity on Friday is the test, assessing what students learned from the lecture and the textbook but nothing from the "library" activity. The library activity was a goose egg—the tenth goose egg in fact. It has been a test of whether a student can find a fact and then copy it from one place to another: a first lesson in plagiarism.

Story Two:

Teacher Y usually spends three weeks on bird ecosystems. The first two weeks are filled with textbook/lecture activities. On Friday of the second week, the teacher announces that the next week will be used to do a library research paper. It has been difficult to get the class scheduled every day in the library for a week, but our teacher has planned ahead and gotten on the calendar.

On Monday, the assignment is given. "Pick a topic having to do with birds you are interested in and write a six-page report." During the research time in the library, the teacher has the librarian conduct the class but is available for questions while grading papers in the corner.

Andrew, one of the students in the class, has had this kind of assignment before and knows exactly what to do so that he can spend most of his library time flirting with Theressa, his latest flame. He seats himself at a library computer and finds that the Internet is down. No worry, he will connect from home on Thursday night to download a paper from his favorite "term paper site" and turn it in Friday morning. No use sweating this one out, particularly since he has two other papers due the same day and every night is taken up with his part-time job. Andrew doesn't know much about birds, but he knows a lot about searching the Internet (using it to cheat) and succeeding with girls.

Story Three:

Teacher Z has been feeling the pressure of both the state standards and the standardized testing and is trying to find a way to cover more material in the same amount of time. Needing more time to focus student attention on what will be tested, the library bird units of the past are cancelled, in favor of parsing sentences.

Our three scenarios are stereotypical but all too common. As a reader, you probably have lived through something similar when you were a student. Perhaps you have taught a bird unit at one time or another.

We propose the banning of goose egg—non-helpful—bird units as low-level learning experiences. They are counter-productive in today's emphasis on achievement and boring, boring, boring to students. To cut out the library experience, however, is no solution at all.

P.S. We have nothing against birds!

What do you mean by "Information-rich and technology-rich environments?"

Permit us a bit of background.

Start with a teacher. Millions of children in the world today have very limited information systems to educate them. They have the wisdom and learning of their parents and their communities, but have only a teacher for more formal education: no fancy facilities, no books, no blackboards, no computers, no desks. To these students, the sum total of information is in the head of their teacher. As a result, rote learning is the primary activity of the school day.

Add a textbook. Millions of other children draw not only upon their culture and their teacher, but have the advantage of a textbook as an added information system. Textbooks have been wonderful inventions because they combine the expertise of many subject specialists coalesced through the eyes of a textbook author into a very versatile data storage mechanism. These information packages are very convenient and available for use both in and out of school, depending on the circumstances and affluence of the school.

The problem with the textbook culture as an information system is now becoming a major challenge. The textbooks of today
- Are often bloated, as the amount of knowledge in many disciplines explodes.
- In addition to core knowledge, all kinds of exercises, side bars, supplementary materials (at additional cost) and every other imaginable resource that a teacher might use, including digital resources available on line.
- Often cost in excess of $100 per copy and weigh so much that parents demand a copy at school and one at home.
- Can only be read by a percentage of the students in the classroom because of low reading level or language problems.
- Are not challenging enough for other students
- Become outdated because of replacement costs
- Often do not correlate well with state standards and state tests.

In the introduction of a recent college textbook, the editor said something to this effect: "All you need to know is in this book and its online supplement of thousands of digitized articles. No need to use the library." An attractive promise indeed. Since the conglomerate publishing company owns many periodicals, publishes many prominent author's works on the topic, and has the capability to deliver its products in any form and at any time, it seems logical to package a total information environment at the highest price the market will bear. From one vantage point, if standards, testing, and the textbook are controlled, then we only have to require teachers to be accountable for the prescribed material. "Here is what to teach. And, here is the schedule of the page you should be teaching from each day of the school year."

Given the problems with the textbook, many have asked: "Isn't there another solution?" While total packaging and regimentation is possible and workable in some countries, it hardly fits the model of a creative and innovative society. We believe that all students would thrive in the next stage of a rich information environment.

Turn on the information-rich and technology-rich environment.
In the eighteenth century, Dennis Diderot felt that the universe contained a finite amount of knowledge and that almost all of what could be known was known. Thus, he created an *Encyclopèdie*, feeling that all knowledge could be captured and summarized in a

single set of volumes. In the late 19th century, Melville Dewey also felt that his classification system would go through only a few editions before it could classify the sum total of all knowledge. The Dewey Decimal System is now in its 22nd edition and is being revised regularly to keep up with the expanding knowledge of the world.

With the introduction of the microcomputer and the Internet in the last decade of the 20th century, the world of information has changed dramatically. Suddenly the information pool has deepened to an ocean, and access through technology is ubiquitous. Schools are making progress toward wireless access—even Starbucks has hot spots. In such an information environment, everything changes, or at least needs to.

What is an information-rich environment?

The illustration here details the components of information-rich and technology-rich environments, as we know them today. This evolves, of course, as various technologies and delivery systems evolve.

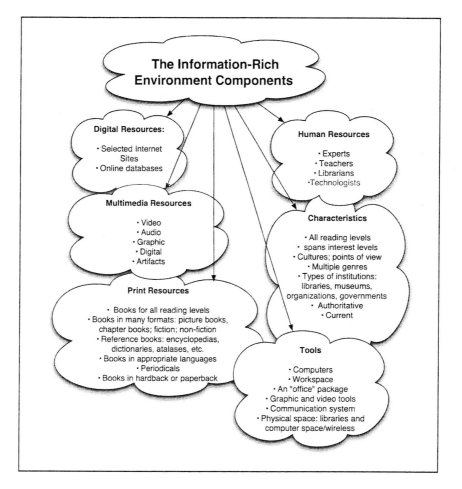

What do we know about the Internet in its decade of major expansion?
- It has billions of sites and may crash under its own glut.
- Contains anything anyone wants to put up including pornography, advertising, chat spots of nefarious characters, and information from any kook who cares to post.
- Allows organizations of all types to post their official information or misinformation.
- Has become a powerful political tool around the world
- Contains more misinformation than accurate data.
- Is becoming outdated as sites are not kept up.
- Is becoming less and less "free" as authors try to recoup their costs of creation and maintenance.
- Is so overloaded with noise from unwanted email and other propaganda that its burden on the individual is almost unbearable.

More importantly, what DOESN'T the Internet contain?
- Almost all copyrighted materials, because authors expect to be paid for their work.
- Almost all fiction and nonfiction books published in the last 75 years—in other words, everything you'd expect to find in a Barnes and Noble.
- Virtually all children's literature published in the last 75 years
- Full-text articles in most magazines and newspapers.

However, FOR A FEE, one can access through the invisible Internet:
- Full-text magazine articles and newspapers, some extending back into the 1980s.
- Current audio books.
- Current music.
- Major databases critical for students and teachers.
- More and more digitized e-books (current copyrighted books usually in PDF format).
- Thousands of term papers and reports ready to download and turn in to a teacher.

And you thought the Internet was free. Well, there's Shakespeare, along with many of the other classics. And there's plenty of stuff at least a century old. But if you want current research, it's going to cost precious shekels.

Yes, I know we are in an information-rich and technology-rich environment, but what is your point?

The point is, in the last twenty years, teaching in a sparse information environment or in a textbook/lecture culture has become antiquated. The real world, and the world our students will live in for the foreseeable future, is a very information-rich and technology-rich world of information. Continuing to teach in an outmoded information space is to continue to use horse and buggy technology in the space age.

The following chart contrasts both poor and rich information environments.

Tightly Controlled and Smaller Information Environment	An Information-Rich and Technology-Rich Information Environment
Advantages: • Everyone on the same page at the same time. • Easy to tally "what has been covered."	Advantages: • Information and technology for each learner at their skill level/language level. • Interest level easier to satisfy. • Variety in itself a motivator. • Simulates the real world of work and life in general. • Can stimulate all learning styles.
Disadvantages: • Learners not on the level of the textbook/lecture/assign-ments. • Satisfies only one learning style.	Disadvantages: • May get out of control. • Usually takes more time if not planned well.

Our second point is that few curriculum leaders, policymakers, school administrators, and teachers have taken any notice. True, we have spent billions on hooking kids up the Internet and turning it on, but we have paid less attention to what's on the wires than the wires themselves.

What do you mean, "education has not taken notice?"

Consider our observations and challenge them if you can:

- National standards for the various curricular areas—such as social studies, science, or math—may refer to the need for computers but either ignore the issue or assume that a high quality information system will be provided.
- Programs at national professional educational associations rarely have sessions addressing how to teach or learn in the new information-rich environments. There are often sessions on how to use a piece of technology in teaching as a useful tool in information access, but rarely on what to do after the button has been pushed and the result is 7,254 web sites available on your topic.
- Few major authors in educational pedagogy take note that the world of information has changed. For example, a major book[1] on building background knowledge never recognized the new information world.
- Major movements, such as Understanding by Design,[2] have great pedagogical ideas. However, we must apply those ideas to the information-rich world where they would flourish.

To educators in information professions, the dismissal of the new world of information has been mystifying on one hand and saddening on another. It is as if the world changed but no one noticed.

Yes, but isn't the movement into this new information and technology environment implied by all the major educational thinkers?

Perhaps. But we are unconvinced that the main players really have considered the major shift in information and really have taken it seriously. We rarely see instructional models that help teachers and students live and work in anything other than a textbook environment or a contained classroom with perhaps a single connection to the Internet or a couple of hundred books in the classroom library. Do a survey yourself. Check any of your popular books in education and look in the index for words like *information, information literature, information skills, library, librarian, databases, Internet,* or any techniques that work only in high quality information environments.

---

[1] *Building Background Knowledge for Academic Achievement: Research on What Works in Schools.* Robert J. Marzano.
[2] Fill in

So What?

There is a presumption that there is a library in the school with rich resources; that there are databases and high quality Internet sites selected for student use; and that these resources are available anywhere and at any time. In today's frantic funding scene, anything taken for granted is likely to disappear. Many school libraries have a very small budget and have not kept up in technology. Often, if a professional retires or moves, a clerk replaces the professional, as if a person with little educational background could build the kind of information system students and teachers desperately need.

Yes, there are stereotypical librarians who protect their ancient books and act like a dictator in their space. Yes, there are tech directors who act like demigods keeping everyone off their networks lest they crash. Those folks need to change or leave. Our point is that without competent professionals who are teachers in both libraries and tech centers, teachers and kids will suffer. In other words, we ignore libraries and tech centers at our own peril. Teachers and administrators who have experienced super school libraries and technology programs have experienced the great lift that quality programs have – non only on the collaborative design of teaching, but the impact these programs have on student learning. It is not surprising that quality school library media programs keep turning up in research studies as making a difference in academic achievement.[3] For those who have not experienced these types of programs, search out and visit several to discover why they make the difference they claim. It's the same everywhere in education. It's people who make the difference.

Again, what's your point?

The premise of this book is that there are three teaching environments, which are all very different:
1. Teaching when there is nothing other than the teacher's knowledge;
2. Teaching in a textbook/lecture world;
3. Teaching in an information-rich and technology-rich environment.

The design of a learning experience and what works in each of the three environments is quite different. Our point is that all pedagogy must be

---

[3] Since 1993, at least fifteen state studies have been conducted identifying quality school library media programs as one component contributing to academic achievement. Many of the studies have been conducted by Ketih Curry Lance in states such as Colorado, Minnesota, Iowa, Illinois, Pennsylvania, Alaska, etc. For a complete list of the studies and their findings, visit http://www.davidvl.org and look for the research link. Or visit the Colorado State Library web site for an additional bibliography of research studies on the impact of school libraries.

redesigned or reinvented to work as the information and technology environment evolves. This will take good librarians and technology specialists to get the job done. Take the case of differentiation of instruction, a concept that is very popular. How can a teacher hope to meet the needs of every child in the classroom when only a few can understand the textbook? Do we assume the teacher is resourceful enough to compensate for a failing information system? Are we forced back into the teaching-by-rote era? Do we assume that the lecture will compensate for the tough textbook? Do we assume that children who are just learning English will understand the lecture? Do we just say to the teacher, "Speak more slowly and loudly and they will understand?" We hardly think any of those suggestions are realistic in a world expecting every child to succeed.

So what do you propose?

First, lets get a few things straight.

- A well-prepared lecture is hard to beat as a teaching technique, although a certain percentage of the students will either ignore it, not understand it, misinterpret it, or try to copy it all down since they expect to be tested on it.
- Textbooks and their supplemental materials are often useful outlines of what should be known and help teachers to structure learning over time. However, they are bloated, too expensive, and usually written for a different audience than "my class."
- Teaching in an information-rich and technology-rich environment is quite different than the textbook/lecture strategy, BUT IT IS THE ONLY HOPE IF ALL STUDENTS ARE GOING TO BE GIVEN AN EQUAL SHAKE.

We propose that each of the three major information environments be recognized by the major instructional designers in education and that teachers be trained to operate in each of these different worlds. Teachers should be taught to recognize the shift in information and technology environments and gain a repertoire of teaching and learning strategies that work best in each. This is no different than the flexibility we expect teachers to master as they confront different learning styles, different student sophistication levels, and the myriad rules and regulations for handling all types of students in an educational organization. It is another dimension to their flexibility, but it is an important one.

But isn't an information-rich and technology-rich environment expensive?

Yes. But compared to the expenditures every year on textbooks, it is very reasonable. Currently, spending for library materials and databases around the U.S. average around $20 per student per year with states like California averaging about $1.00 and others spending upwards of $30.00 Expenditures on technology hardware vary widely from state to state and district to district. Initially, spending for technology was substantial, but as time has passed and budgets have shrunk, many districts have cut back dramatically. It is certain that many administrators often budget for hardware and educational software, but skimp on the information to go on the wires. Thus, librarians and technology specialists struggle to provide as much quality information as they can with limited funds.

Quality collections of materials can be maintained under $25 a year per student. What a bargain! For the price of a single hardback book in a typical bookstore, students are beginning to taste a quality information system. We often give librarians the guideline that one book a year per student will maintain a collection, but the price of two books per year will be needed to keep collections of print, multimedia, and digital collections fresh. If we were to provide equitable spending for textbooks and the information system we are describing, spending for library budgets would have to quadruple in most districts and be increased a hundred fold in a state like California (more about this when we discuss our vision of the future).

More and more information—particularly databases and online periodicals—require schools to treat information as a utility. That is, if the bill is not paid, access to the database is cut off. School districts are going to have to learn that paying the information bill is akin to paying the electric bill. No power, no school. No information, no school. To turn off both is to retreat quickly into the 19th century—hardly a place where we'd like our 21st century children, who are supposed to be the best and brightest in the world, to be educated.

But even if we fund the information-rich environment, aren't kids lost in such a vast space?

Admittedly, students can surf, fiddle, and waste a great deal of time paddling around in information space so that in a normal hour of research they would not really get anything done except wandering.

The librarians of the nation have come up with a model to help students and teachers navigate a broad information space. Their strategy is to teach information literature and advocate that students who use the real world of information should be information literate. Information literacy is defined not only as finding information, but also as evaluating it very carefully before using it to build knowledge or do a task. Whereas librarians traditionally concentrated on helping patrons find information, their task has now switched to helping patrons judge, analyze, and use information.

We can all probably remember the days when we were doing research in the library and used the *Reader's Guide to Periodical Literature* to help us find magazines. We would laboriously copy out 20 citations, take them to the magazine room, and hope to find at least one that we could cite. Today, we type in a search term and are overwhelmed with information on our topic. It requires information literature skills to know what to use and whether it is worth using at all.

Librarians often teach the research process adapted from the scientific method. Below is a generic model of the process librarians teach as students confront a problem in an information-rich environment.

The Information Literacy Process

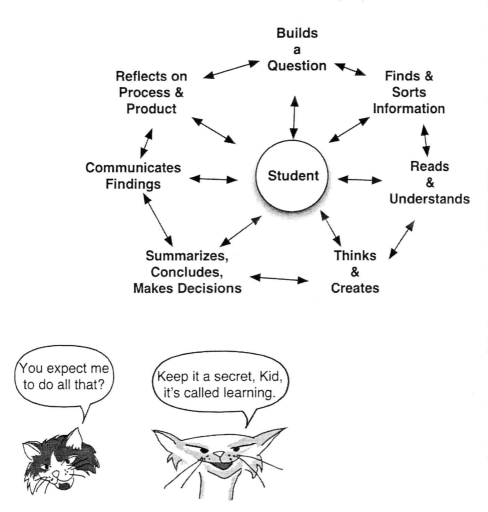

If you ask any librarian about information literacy and what they are trying to accomplish above and beyond the old library skills (of learning the Dewey Decimal System and reading catalog cards), expect an earful.

Enough of that! What are the 15 models for teaching and learning that are spoken about in the title of the book?

We created 15 models to teach and learn when information abounds based on our long experience with learners and study of many research reports spanning education, library science, and technology.

We divided these models into three categories:
1. Appetizers
2. The Main Course
3. Dessert

Appetizers are fairly simple models and can be used easily within many other teaching strategies. The main course models might be the entire structure of a total learning experience. Dessert challenges the teacher to use all the models creatively as the occasion presents itself.

The models do not work well in an information-poor environment but are structured in such a way that students will have lots of choices in information, multimedia, and human resources. Here are our assumptions about the models as a whole:

- The models do not ask teachers to discard any effective teaching technique that already works.

- Each model requires the student not just to cut, clip, or extract information from a wide variety of sources, but to use higher-level thinking strategies to accomplish the learning objective.

- The models demand that information and technology gurus (often known as librarians and technology specialists) collaborate with the teacher in designing learning.

- The models require every "bird unit" to be redesigned. Redesign is often a simple but very important tweak.

- The models require every school give more than lip service to the creation of a high-quality information system usually known as the library—but a library of very different proportions to the old one that stored a few tattered volumes and was visited once a week for a story and a "library lesson." Such new libraries cost a substantial amount of money and not only have print materials, but also have the digital school library system that is available 24 hours a day, seven days a week from anywhere in the world a student happens to be.

- The models assume that the librarian and/or the technology specialist do more than just keep the wires or sort the books. They are either willing to participate in designing quality learning experiences, or their jobs are shifted to another spot in education.

- Not all learning experiences need to take place in an information-rich environment. It is quite appropriate to rely totally on a teacher's experience or totally on a textbook/lecture format at times, but never as a steady diet. Variety is the spice of education and will likely lift boredom and increase motivation as expectations for learning are raised.

- Just because the information environment expands, the time for teaching a topic need not expand. It may, as students get immersed in a fascinating learning experience, but not always.

- None of the models are mandated in their exact form. Rather, they should be used with other creative ideas and judged on their impact on the amount learned in the time available.

- None of the models cast the total burden for teaching on a single individual, but presume that both the teacher and partner specialists be in the saddle to cut the teacher/pupil ratio at least in half. The notion is that two heads are better than one. All models presume collaborative planning, team teaching and joint assessment of the learning.

Perhaps a few examples would help here.

As you scan the list of models below and read the tweaks suggested, you might catch a brief glimpse of what we are talking about. Expanded examples accompanying each of the models in the main section will flesh out these ideas.

Examples of Higher Level Bird Units

Model	Sample approaches for information-rich environments
Appetizers	
1.Background to Question Model	Birding with digital cameras. Examine feathers under a microscope. Visit a bird sanctuary, museum, or art gallery.
2.Sensemaking Model	Research migration and create visual maps, charts, or graphs. Discover things that birds can do that are replicated in technology, and create a visual display (e.g. beaks-nutcracker or straw, claws-hooks or vice grip).
3. Read, View, Listen Model	Explore books, videos, or websites to discover: What are birds used for? What uses are harmful? What do legends and myths tell us about birds in different cultures? Read stories having a wise old owl character and discover the common characteristics.
4. Advice to Action Model	Consult expert advice on how to attract birds to the schoolyard and your own backyard.
5. Compare & Contrast Model	Research and compare: swamp birds and desert birds, nocturnal birds and diurnal birds, woodpeckers and hummingbirds, two birds with webbed feet such as a Canada goose and a puffin..., the structure and function of wings of birds and airplanes, or pigeons around the world.
The Main Course	
6. Concept Jigsaw Model	How has art been influenced by birds? Examine painting, sculpture, plays, ballet, music, movies, or poetry.
7. Problems/ Possibilities Jigsaw Puzzle Model	Which birds are threatened or endangered? How can we protect them?
8. Matrix Model	Are all oviparous animals birds?
9. Timeline Model	Explore the evolution of birds. Document the history of ornithology. Hatch eggs in the classroom and document the process. Show location of a migratory bird, such as a hummingbird, during the period of a year.
10. History & Mystery Model	'Winged Man" How were early flying machines influenced by birds?
11. Take a Position Model	Do we need an international agreement to conserve and manage bird populations?
12. Recreate Model	Role-play waterfowl migrating from their nesting habitat in the far North to their wintering grounds in the South.
13. Re-invent a Better Way Model	Build a birdhouse or birdbath, paper airplane, or a peanut birdfeeder that squirrels can't eat from.
14. The Quest	Do a major study of birds whether in the form of an I-Search Paper, a formal research paper, a major WebQuest, or other sizeable research project.
Dessert	
15. Mix It Up	Combine any of the models above creatively

What are the techniques that would help teachers the most in applying these models?

In many instances, the tweaks applied to create higher-level learning experiences are not just the groupings or structure of the model but the ability to ask good questions. A good question will be interesting and relevant to the students and will sustain that interest or curiosity throughout the learning experience. This is critical, since all the models will require the students to think harder and do more work than they would during a passive unit. A good question will not be able to be answered by cutting and clippings answers from an information source. A student will not be able to find their work already done for them from some website or reference book. The question will cause them to combine various information sources, think about the information, and build a fresh perspective, idea, or reject everything they have encountered and be truly creative. For ideas on how to build better questions consult Jamie McKenzie's work at http://www.fno.org/sept96/questions.html

A second technique that will boost the likelihood of success is the teaching of group dynamics during the unit. All the 15 models can begin with individuals, but invariably end up in some kind of grouping as information is pooled, analyzed, and synthesized. Since teams or groups are so common in our workforce in laboratories, commercial enterprises, or many organizational structures, teaching group skills is a life skill that may as well be mastered early.

But are the models based on research?

It is true that the development of the models rests squarely on a body of professional experience. The authors have a combined experience of over 75 years in the United States and Canada. Together they have worked with teachers at all grade levels and in all disciplines; they have worked with librarians and technology directors across the continent; and they have spoken to educators at professional conferences and workshops in every province of Canada and in almost every state of the U.S.

But beyond that experience comes the support of research studies across the field of education. One of the authors conducted an extensive review of the literature of information literacy across the world[4]. All the models are based in research reviews done by Robert J. Marzano,[5] and others in the

---

[4] Loertscher, David V. and Blanche Woolls. *Information Literacy: a Review of the Research.* 2nd ed. Hi Willow Research & Publishing, 2002.

[5] Our favoriie works of Robert Marzano include his *What Works Series* published by ASCD. Individual titles are listed in the resources section at the end of this book.

Understanding by Design movement.[6] We have also used reviews of research in technology[7] and reviews of reading research done by Krashen and McQuillan.[8] The work here has been affected by much of the literature in higher-level thinking, creativity, and the work in inquiry and constructivist education.[9] This is true because the best ideas in education today link into an information-rich environment.

Much of the skills-based approach to education is not a part of our foundation because the best of those techniques work better in a predominantly closed information system. We don't see that the practice of math facts—whether in the dirt with a stick, on the chalkboard, using a set of flash cards, or being presented with problems on the computer—is any different. The information space is equally narrow and appropriate for drill and practice. It makes little difference whether early learning of the piano is done on a $20,000 Steinway grand piano or on a $30 electronic keyboard. Thus, we have not been impressed with the body of technology research that has tried to compare learning the same facts, operations, or ideas via computer, written text, oral lecture, or any other comparative medium. Those studies have generally come out with "no significant differences" and we have not been surprised. It is not so important that technology delivers the same information that is in a book or a magazine; it is the fact that technology can deliver information in a myriad of different ways, in different sophistication levels, in varying genres, and with differentiation as its key strength. We do admire the efforts of a number of national organizations to promote technology in ways that truly enhance learning.[10]

[6] Wiggins & McTigue. Understanding By Design. ASCD, 1999. And Understanding By Design Handbook. ASCD, 2004.

[7] Center for Applied Research in Educational Technology (CARET) at: http://caret.iste.org/

[8] Krashen, Stephen. The Power of Reading. 2nd ed. Lib raries Unlimited, 2004.

[9] See our list of favorite titles in the resources section at the end of the book.

[10] Our favorites include: the Partnership for 21st Century Skills at http://21stcenturyskills.org/; The George Lucas Educational Foundation (GLEF) that publishes Edutopia at http://www.glef.org/; The various standards documents published by the International Society for Technology in Education (ISTE) at http://www.iste.org/ and the enGauge 21st Century Skills project at http://www.ncrel.org/engauge/skills/skills.htm

If you authors had your wish, what would a likely scenario be for education in an information-rich and technology-rich environment?

Since you asked, here is a picture of a restructured school that we think would work.

1. Start with an information ticket. For every day a student is in school, the federal government would supply a $5.00 information ticket. Thus, if a student moved from school to school, the current school would claim the money. If a child were home schooled, a public library or a school that agreed to provide the information support might claim the ticket. In no case would a single commercial entity be allowed to claim the information ticket (although they would be happy to do so).
   a. A $5.00 bill per day would pay for the following information services:
      i. $2.00 - All textbooks and accompanying consumables selected locally.
      ii. $1.00 - A library, both print and digital, including online databases, groups of carefully selected web sites, and multimedia selected locally. The digital portion would be available 24/7 and from any location worldwide.
      iii. $2.00 - A connection device (perhaps a cross between a PDA and a notebook computer and one that would last two years and then exchanged for an upgraded model).

   The ticket would not pay for additional equipment, the wireless network system itself, or the salaries of the persons administering the system. In other words, like a utility such as gas or electric, the information system would be a basic component of the education system rather than an add-on as at present. Benevolent funding has never worked and never will.

2. Create an educational pod of four teachers and their normal quota of students. This group of four would have the following structure
   a. A knowledge team leader qualified as an information/technology/ curriculum/instructional designer
   b. Three regularly-credentialed teachers

Such a team could be generalists, as elementary teachers are, and would have the same children for several years. Or, the team could be four specialists such as social studies, science, math, or fine arts, and students would rotate among the various pods of specialists.

The focus would be on the knowledge team leader who would spend approximately half the day in planning and assessment and half the day teaming with one or the entire group on educational units.

The knowledge team leader would have the following qualifications and training:

    a. Credentials as a master teacher before being allowed to apply for the job.
    b. Advanced coursework in instructional and curriculum design.
    c. Competence in information—selection, acquisition, use, and the teaching of information literacy from library and information science.
    d. Expertise in the use of technology as an educational tool
    e. Management and leadership competencies.

In Summary

We can't help but agree with the Committee on Developments in the Science of Learning in their expanded edition of *How People Learn*:[11]

> More than ever, the sheer magnitude of human knowledge renders its coverage by education as an impossibility; rather, the goal of education is better conceived as helping students develop the intellectual tools and learning strategies needed to acquire the knowledge that allows people to think productively about history, science and technology, social phenomena, mathematics and the arts. Fundamental understanding about subjects including how to frame and ask meaningful questions about various subject areas, contributes to individuals' more basic understanding of basic principles learning that can assist them in becoming self-sustaining life-long learners (p.5).

We believe that the models in this book provide effective strategies for teaching and learning in an information-rich environment rather than being crushed by information overload. Feedback to the authors is appreciated and can be addressed to David V. Loertscher at davidl@slis.sjsu.edu

---

[11] *How People Learn: Brain, Mind, Experience, and School.* Expanded Edition. National Academic Press, 2004 Created by the Committee on Developments in the Science of Learning, Commission on Behavioral and Social Sciences and Education, National Research Council.

A Few Notes for Librarians

Rivaling the "heartbreak of psoriasis" is the amassing of books, digital information, and multimedia and then having few customers. For half a century, school librarians have begged, cajoled, and smooth-talked monies to build resources for teaching and learning. And national standards have placed collaborative teaching and learning as a top priority in boosting achievement. The potential to contribute to teaching and learning has never been greater.

As the authors travel about North America, the number one complaint we hear from school librarians is that teachers are either unwilling or too busy to collaborate. And when they do, the "bird unit" ideas predominate. Our message in a world interested only in the bottom line of scores has been that the time has come to "strut our stuff."

Teaching and learning in an information-rich and technology-rich environment holds a great deal of promise because this environment is the real world of the 21st century. Armed with that knowledge, the authors have created models to replace the annoying and low-level library activities that are all too commonplace across the continent.

It is one thing to ban bird units from the library; it is quite another to have exciting alternatives that truly boost understanding and achievement. Teachers often avoid libraries because of time constraints, but they also fear that time spent doing research or encountering anything except what is tested will negatively affect scores. Furthermore, many librarians find that the time they have to collaborate is being cut as clerical help diminishes or as jobs are cut from full to part time.

The concern of administrators to economize by eliminating professional librarians but keeping the library open through clericals or volunteers presumes that access alone makes the difference. "If we just keep the computers plugged in, the books on the shelf, and the door open, it is sufficient." If this reasoning were used for the management of the principal's office or the classroom, where would the school be? The professionals in the library play as significant a role as principals and teachers.

The authors are often asked which is better: "to have a teacher bring a class to the library doing low-level learning activities or not come at all?" We recommend the latter as shocking as that may seem. Our advice to every librarian is to link arms with principals and forward-thinking teachers in a resolve to maximize the contribution that the library makes to achievement. There is no time to allow nonsense or vacation time in the library. Librarians cannot claim a contribution to teaching and learning unless literacy and understanding are being built day in and day out.

The models presented in this book are, in reality, tweaks to good teaching practices. Their message is not that everything done previously is wrong and that our models are the only right way. Rather, they are that little extra boost that can push a learning activity to successful completion—to win the race, not merely participate in it. Experience with the models indicates that librarians go through two stages: first, the slavish application of a particular model to build repertoire. Second, librarians become creative at combining parts of models as they watch and gauge student learning, motivation, and excitement for the library.

It is impossible to improve or fine-tune "the dreaded worksheet" exercise. Copying facts from one location to another and passing them in or merely regurgitating them is counterproductive no matter how it is framed or implemented. It matters not whether the fact has been copied with a pencil or cut and pasted by computer. It is all the same nonsense.

For doubters, we recommend viewing the video "We are Information Literate!" available from LMC Source at http://www.lmcsource.com. When first graders experience high-level learning experiences and then are interviewed as fifth graders, what differences can a single learning experience replicated at each grade level make? As authors, we are convinced that given whatever time the librarian has to collaborate, it is more important to do a few model learning experiences than many mediocre ones.

Because excellence is its own reward, the challenge of experimenting, creating, honing, tweaking, and elevating learning experiences in libraries is worth accepting. And, it's all part of earning our keep and perhaps an extreme makeover of what libraries contribute to learning.[12]

---

[12] See: Loertscher, David V. "Extreme Makeover." *School Library Journal*, November, 2004.

Part One

Appetizers:

1. Background to Question Model
2. Sensemaking Model
3. Read, View, and Listen Model
4. Advice to Action Model
5. Compare and Contrast Model

Background to Question Model

Background to Question Model

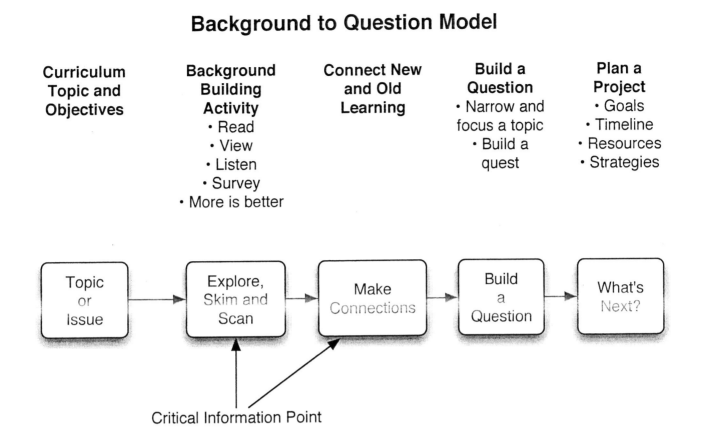

Curriculum Topic and Objectives	Background Building Activity	Connect New and Old Learning	Build a Question	Plan a Project
	• Read • View • Listen • Survey • More is better		• Narrow and focus a topic • Build a quest	• Goals • Timeline • Resources • Strategies

Topic or Issue → Explore, Skim and Scan → Make Connections → Build a Question → What's Next?

Critical Information Point

Why This Model?

• Compensate for uneven prior knowledge
• Use when prior knowledge is skimpy
• Help learners build engaging questions when they seem to lack interest
• Provide an opportunity for a "topic to select a learner"
• Use when the textbook is insufficient
• Help learners narrow a topic when struggling with generalities
• Turn a library orientation into an exploration

Possible Topics:

• Environmental issues
• Genetics
• Health and safety issues
• Political ideologies
• Types of music
• Science fair projects
• Pet care and needs
• Media influence on behavior
• Marine biology
• Rain forests
• Middle Ages
• Middle East
• Early settlers
• Ecosystems

Critical Information Literacy Skills*

• Explore a Topic, K&Z, p. 4
• Search Strategies, K&Z p. 24
• Locate Resources, K&Z p 26
• Select Relevant Data, K&Z p. 62
• Skim, Scan, Consider, K&Z, p. 32
• Make Connections, K&Z p. 116
• Reflect, Transfer, Apply, K&Z p. 166
• Develop Questions, K&Z p. 12
• Define a Research Topic, K&Z p. 8

* Koechlin, Carol and Sandi Zwaan. *Build Your Own Information Literate School.* Hi Willow, 2003

Notes on Background to Question Model

"Let's start at the very beginning; a very good place to start" sings Maria in *The Sound of Music*. Analogously, we must get every runner (learner) to the starting line for the main event (the unit to come). On any topic, students' knowledge will vary along the continuum. Often their past experiences and opportunities will influence the extent of their prior knowledge of the topic. Our job is to prepare each student for a successful engagement with the topic by drawing on what background information they have and assisting them to build the additional source knowledge they need. Whether our students are all English speakers or English learners; whether they come from rich or poor backgrounds; whether they have traveled the world or never been five miles from home, the background model can be used effectively to level the playing field and raise general knowledge before launching into a major learning experience. Imagine what might happen if we introduced the following topics without assessing students' background knowledge.

- "Our topic today is differential equations" (blank stare)
- "We will be comparing the cases of war in the 19th and the 20th centuries" (blank stare).
- "We will be studying the history of California "(half blank stares if announced in San Diego where the children are not sure of the country they live in).

To launch forward, particularly when we know that most of the children in the classroom cannot read the textbook, is asking for failure. It would be wise to spend a class period, an entire day, or even a couple of days bringing everyone to the same general background understanding.

Before beginning you may need to:
- Define the type of background knowledge the learner is expected to know.
- Assemble materials of all types and kinds:
    - Books of pictures with a minimum of text
    - Easy-reading articles in encyclopedias, children's books (good even up into high school), reference books such as atlases, subject dictionaries—particularly those that add word descriptions
    - Video tapes to view in whole or just in clips
    - Books to read aloud before the unit begins (such as historical fiction or strong information books with interesting narrative)
    - Internet sites at the kid level
    - A virtual or real field trip
    - A good speaker who can explain or dramatize a topic
    - Culturally diverse materials
    - Charts, maps graphs, illustrations
    - Artifacts
- Decide on the location for the background building activity: the classroom if materials and technology can be assembled there; the library if the richest variety of materials and technology is desired.

The information-rich and technology-rich environment provides many opportunities to skim and scan, boost interest, increase motivation, and differentiate for every learner in the classroom. Here are a few suggestions:

- Read a book aloud before the unit begins.
- Set up stations with various types of materials the learners can preview.
- Set aside time to use the materials. This could be during the regular SSR time and/or special times in the library.
- As students skim and scan, propose vocabulary lists for the entire class, have them keep notes on what they read, and create visual representations of their notes (see the worksheet in this section).
- Start building questions that will develop into essential questions of the unit to come.
- Have students nominate resources that will be helpful later in the full-blown unit.
- Have learners create a concept map before they begin and add to their map as they skim and scan.
- Skim and scan as many materials in the time available.
- Build vocabulary lists on the board as skimming and scanning happens.
- Share what is being learned in pairs or small groups.
- Encourage every student to follow up on their curiosity or on genres they discover and have enjoyed.
- Continue the background-building activity as long as interest and progress toward the starting line is progressing.

For students with poor background knowledge, this activity is their ONLY HOPE of succeeding in the main event. Best of all, expectations for learning in the main unit of instruction can be raised. Students will be prepared for their trip to a museum, be ready for the enactment of the Seder meal, will have participated in building questions they want to explore, and best of all, may have actually developed interest in the topic.

Technology

Use the following exploring technologies for the background-building activity:

- Playback technologies for videotapes, DVDs, streaming video, audio playback, etc.
- If learners are to search for their materials, then the library catalog, Internet searching techniques, and database search engines will need to be taught and available on location. Ask the librarian to teach the needed search and sorting strategies. Otherwise, students will waste a great deal of time surfing but not finding.
- If searching and sorting time is minimal, then supply the materials so that reading, viewing, and listening time is maximized.

Research

The best arguments for building background knowledge including a summary of the research is in Robert J. Marzano's *Building Background Knowledge for Academic Achievement* (ASCD, 2004).

Critical Information Skills for Background to Question Model

Explore a Topic
Students will use a variety of strategies to explore a topic in preparation for research.

This first step in research is crucial to research success. Students are often discouraged by research projects because they find the topic too broad, too narrow or of no personal interest. Engage students and fire up their passion and curiosity. Provide them with a good working knowledge of the topic so they can create questions, select effective keywords and become familiar with the language of the topic.

Sort
Students will sort gathered data for specific purposes

Sorting is an important entry-level analysis skill. Provide students with tactile/concrete sorting experiences before tackling the sorting of data (e.g. sort pictures, books, stamps, etc.). Before students begin to sort, clear purpose and criteria must be established.

Classify
Students will classify data gathered for specific purposes.

Classifying formalizes the sorting process by applying a system or principle. This high level activity is a very important skill that information users need to understand. All information sources (e.g. non-fiction books, specialized encyclopedias, newspapers, videos, Web Sites etc.) are structured or organized using a system or principle. Experiences with sorting and classifying data will help students to understand how to find information when they need it.

Make Connections
Students will work with information to make connections.

There are many "connection building" strategies we can teach to help students understand content. When we suggest that students make connections we want them to make links to what they already know; what they know about the topic, what they know about reading (viewing/listening) strategies, what they know about webbing/mapping, and how this new content fits into their personal experiences.

Develop Questions
Students will develop effective questions to guide their research.

Research is the question. Successful research projects are dependant on the quality of the question(s). To think critically about a topic, students need to develop effective questions to guide them in the research process. They need questions that drive analysis. The secret to developing good research questions is to provide students with rich exploratory experiences so they have a solid background to think and wonder about. Helping students to become more conscious of the kinds of questions they can formulate and helping them to realize which questions will generate high-level critical thinking is the next challenge.

Develop a Plan
Students will analyze the elements of the assignment, develop a plan and implement it.

Ultimately we want students to be able to independently analyze a task and develop a personal plan of action. A Research Plan; provides a learning map, keeps everything organized, keeps you on task, helps meet assessment criteria, chunks the process, sets target dates.

Examples of Background to Question Model

Unit 1: An Extraterrestrial's Guide to Finding Our School (Prelude to a State Study)   Gr. 3–6

Goal: To create a wall-sized map to guide an extraterrestrial from our solar system to our planet, to our continent, to our country, to our state, to the many things it will find in our state, to our city, and finally to our school.

Explore, Skim and Scan: Students gather all the information, pictures, places, drawings, and technology they will need to construct their massive map. Learners extract all the information they will need and prepare the various maps to begin their map making.

Map-Making: Various groups are assigned portions of the map: one group creates a picture of the solar system with an arrow to earth; another group draws or prints out a picture of the earth with our continent visible (arrow showing where we are); another group prepares a map of the US with state outlines visible and our state in solid color (arrow points to where we are in the state); another group prepares a large map of the state with mountains, rivers, major cities and our city (arrow pointing to our city); another group has a map of our city posted with an arrow to our school; and, finally, another group has a map of our school building showing where to find our room. Everyone prints out as many pictures of places, natural resources, food, industries or other features to post on or near the maps. Then everyone tries to become a docent to lead the extraterrestrial visitor from outer space to find us in our classroom.

Build Questions: Along the way we build questions based on our interests about our state, town, city, or school that will develop into essential questions as we begin our state history unit.

Unit 2: An Introduction to Bacteria   Gr. 7–9

Topic: We wish to introduce learners to the wonderful world of bacteria through the amazing technology of microphotography. This will spark interest in a major study of the ways bacteria affect our lives and the efforts of science and medicine to control that world.

Resources: Students learn to search out pictures and information about bacteria in books, magazines, and Internet sites.

Skim and Scan: Students spend time collecting and reproducing pictures in print form or in digital images. Next, they make notes to attach to the images, containing name, where found, what they do, whether dangerous to humans or animals, or other interesting tidbits. Finally, they make connections by arranging their pictures in some logical way, whether by shape, location, dangerous or benign, etc.

Build Questions: Students build questions that will emerge as essential questions in their major study of bacteria. The best sources of information have been noted and are saved for future use.

Unit 3: European Explorers Trek to North America   Gr. 4–6

What are the 5 W's of European explorers?

Explore, skim and scan

Students will be studying the impact of European Explorers on North America. The teacher and teacher-librarian realize that the students need to gain some general knowledge of explorers before they embark on their own voyage of discovery. Develop a list of key words students should use for searches. Students have blank *Quick Fact Trading Cards* to complete. They rotate through the resource stations (print encyclopedia, electronic encyclopedia, books, pictures, and video) set up in the library and complete as many cards as possible in the time available. They skim, scan, read, view and listen to variety of carefully selected resources.

Make Connections

Students gather in small groups, and sort their trading cards alphabetically by explorer's last name. They share the quick facts they recorded on their cards and take note of any conflicting data. Have students sort their cards chronologically, by departure point, by destination and reason for the excursion.

Build Questions

Have groups discuss findings and develop questions using the *Question Storming* worksheet. Groups share questions with class. Have students revisit their trading cards, and consider the group questions to help them settle on the aspect of European exploration or the particular explorer(s) they want to investigate. Students create a question for individual study. Introduce the *Question Rubric,* explaining criteria, so students understand how their questions will be evaluated. Provide students with focus words such as impact, effect, results, resulted, relationships, conditions, significance etc. to help them build good inquiry questions.

What's next?

Students refine their inquiry questions in consultation with the teacher or teacher-librarian and develop a plan for their research.

Unit 4: Science Fair Sampler   Gr. 5–8

What can I do for science fair?

Explore, Skim and Scan

The Science Department and the teacher librarian will work together to develop an exploration activity to give students an overview and some background knowledge of potential topics for their Science Fair projects. The exploration activity will spark interest in topics as well as provide orientation to the many resources available to students through the school library. Centers focus on curriculum topics and are arranged by resource types (e.g. science magazines—print and electronic, encyclopedias—print and electronic, books, video and selected web sites). Students rotate through centers and complete reflective prompts on their organizer *Science Fair Exploration*.

Make Connections

Now students need to consider possible topics and questions for their personal science fair projects. Use the organizer *Science Fare: Whetting Your Appetite.* Students complete the columns and think about all these comments as they assign a ranking to their possible topics. Now they review the rankings, select and circle their top three choices, consult with their teacher and decide on the project they want to try.

Build a Question

Review Science Fair criteria with students then have them create a triple T-Chart. Students record their purpose or question and continue to complete the T-chart using the following headings: What do I Know? What do I Need to Find Out? Where can I find Information?

What's Next?

Students develop an action plan. Be sure it includes a materials list and a timeline.

Unit 5: All That Jazz: A Guided E-tour   Gr. 7–11

What is Jazz? Why is it important?

Explore, Skim and Scan

Begin by listening to great jazz CD's, a picture book (e.g. *The Sound of Jazz* by Weatherford and Velasqueq, *If I Only Had a Horn - Young Louis Armstrong* by Roxane Orgill) or a video. Prepare the students to take an etour by following the *Guided Tour* itinerary. Share and discuss the *Etour Rubric* so students understand how their tour will be evaluated. They visit a variety of bookmarked websites to find answers to their Guiding Questions (See *Guided Tour*) and to give them a working knowledge of jazz so that they will be able to engage in a meaningful experience as they do an in-depth study later. Students record brief point form answers on the *Jazz Tour Map* worksheet.

Make Connections

After the tour, gather as a large group to share and discuss findings. Ask students to do a learning log using prompts such as: I was surprised to discover..., It is amazing that..., I wonder..., What if?

Build a Question

Discuss areas of interest and help students develop questions to guide their continued research. Provide them with focus words from which to choose for inclusion in their question. (e.g. influence, impact, effect, relationship, importance, significance) Introduce the *Question Rubric*, explaining criteria, so students understand how their questions will be evaluated.

What's next?

Guide students to create a plan for their individual research, based on their newly formed questions. Their plan should include goals, timelines, resources and strategies.

Gathering Evidence of Understanding
- students navigated sites effectively and stayed on task
- students completed the *Jazz Tour Map* with accurate data
- learning logs indicated students made connections
- questions developed will guide meaningful research about importance of jazz
- research plans are complete and realistic

InfoSkills
- search strategies - search the Internet
- make connections
- develop questions
- make a plan

Reflect, Rethink, Redesign
- Did the beginning activity (CD, book, video) stimulate interest?
- Are there other CD's, books, videos, I could offer to share with interested students during this project?
- Were students enthusiastic about the etour? How could I motivate those who weren't?
- Did students understand the importance of the etour rubric? Could they accurately evaluate their tour based on the rubric?
- Did students experience difficulty creating a good question? Should I be planning more experiences with question development? Would a question matrix help?
- Was the question rubric helpful? Were students able to use it to evaluate their own questions accurately? Were they able to see the weaknesses in their first questions and improve them?
- Did students produce useful realistic plans? Are there students who would benefit from a planning guide or organizer?

Quick Fact Trading Cards

European Explorers
Quick Fact Trading Cards

Who?

What?

When?

Where?

Why?

European Explorers
Quick Fact Trading Cards

Who?

What?

When?

Where?

Why?

European Explorers
Quick Fact Trading Cards

Who?

What?

When?

Where?

Why?

European Explorers
Quick Fact Trading Cards

Who?

What?

When?

Where?

Why?

Question Storming

Write your topic in the centre starburst. Record questions you have about this topic in the surrounding ovals. Continue to develop questions about these questions to further explore and refine your topic.

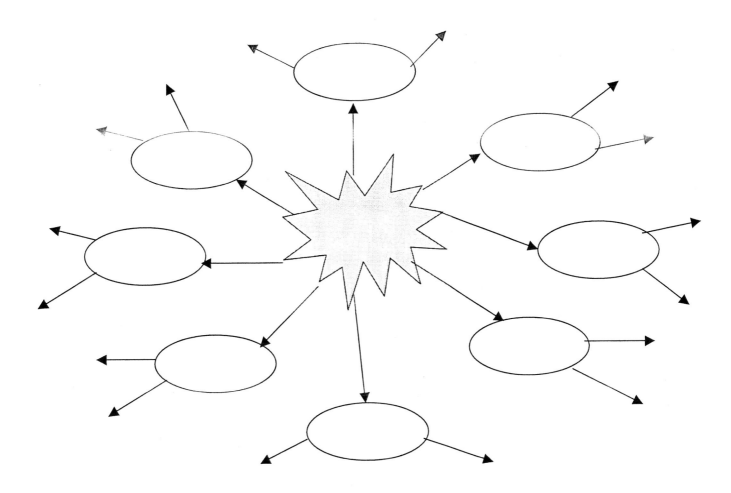

Which questions would you really like to explore for your research project?

Science Fair Exploration

Name:... Class..

Welcome to the library. Today you will be exploring four types of resources to discover topics and ideas that might make interesting science fair projects. At each station, use your skim and scan skills to help you read and view as much material as possible today. Use the organizer to record your thoughts and possible ideas for science fair projects. **Happy hunting!**

Periodical Station (magazines & newspapers) That's interesting... I didn't know that... I want to know more about....	Computer Station That's interesting... I didn't know that... I want to know more about....
Science Books Station That's interesting... I didn't know that... I want to know more about....	Video Station That's interesting... I didn't know that... I want to know more about....

Good Job. When you decide on the focus for your project, come back and visit us again. We can help you find out lots more.

Science Fair: Wetting Your Appetite

Record the all topics you are interested in. Make a note of the things that intrigue you about each topic. Think about the potential pluses and minuses of developing this topic for your science fair project. Think about your timelines, materials, and experience.

Topics of Interest to Me	Intriguing Factors	Positives	Negatives	Rank 1–5
1				
2				
3				
4				
5				
6				
7				
8				
9				
10				

➢ Rank your topics on a scale of 1–5 (1 of little interest, 5 very interesting).

➢ Circle your three most interesting topics.

➢ Consider science fair criteria and conference with your teacher to discuss your ideas.

➢ Pick the topic you will work on and start planning.

Your Research Question - Rubric

Level \ Criteria	Focus	Interest	Knowledge	Processing
Your Research Question:	*Does your question help to focus your research?*	*Are you excited about your question?*	*Will your question help you learn?*	*Will your question help you to understand your topic better?*
Level 4	- will evoke personal reaction	- inspires further investigation and more questions	- catalyst for transfer or application	- requires independent analysis, synthesis and application of information
Level 3	- requires looking at information from a variety of perspectives	- stimulates curiosity and enthusiasm	- directs personal reflection, opinion	- requires general comparison based on criteria
Level 2	- manageable, with limited exploration potential	- motivates some personal interest	- requires collection of facts and opinions	- requires classification of data
Level 1	- broad and unmanageable or narrow with little scope	- of little personal interest	- requires lists, one word answers	- requires data collection only

Adapted from *Info Tasks for Successful Learning*, Pembroke Publishers

Planning a Guided E-tour

Topic:
Essential Question:

Curriculum Expectations and Information Skills

Selected Web Sites

Guiding Questions

Assessment Criteria

E-tour Rubric

Criteria	Background Building	Navigating	Note Taking
Level 4	- accurate and abundant information collected from the tour - effective and efficient use of both itinerary and guiding questions	- navigates to and from relevant web sites with ease - able to return to home page and navigate back and forth in several sites at the same time to make comparisons	- skims and scans to identify relevant information - efficiently selects relevant data and makes effective use of allotted time
Level 3	- accurate and adequate information collected from the tour - information collected indicates guiding questions and itinerary were used effectively	- uses hot links selectively to locate required information - able to return to home page and navigate back and forth	- skims and scans to gain an overview - identifies useful information and makes effective use of time
Level 2	- incomplete or inaccurate information collected from the tour - information collected indicates some of the guiding questions were used and the itinerary was followed loosely	- uses hot links randomly and with limited success - able to use navigation tools with some success	- skims and scans with some success - has difficulty evaluating usefulness of data and runs out of time
Level 1	- little information collected from the tour - paid little attention to either guiding questions and/or itinerary	- shows little understanding of significance of hot links - indicates little or no understanding of navigation tools such as "back" arrow or "home" link	- demonstrates limited ability to skim and scan - fails to evaluate usefulness of data and consequently spends time inefficiently

Guided E-tour

The History of Jazz

Selected Web Sites:

Jazz Hall of Fame
http://www.jazzhall.org/

Hyper Music History of Jazz
http://www.hypermusic.ca/jazz/mainmenu.html

A Passion for Jazz
http://www.apassion4jazz.net/index.html

Jazz a Film by Ken Burns
http://www.pbs.org/jazz/
http://www.artsci-ccwin.concordia.ca/history/Carr_article.html

Music Making History: Africa Meets Europe in the United States of the Blues
http://asweknowit.ca/evcult/USBlues.shtml

The Red Hot Jazz Archive
http://asweknowit.ca/evcult/USBlues.shtml

The Golden Age of Jazz
http://www.jazzphotos.com/

Planet Jazz Magazine
http://www.planetjazzmagazine.ca/

Louisiana State Museum: Audio Jazz Glossary
http://lsm.crt.state.la.us/site/audio/glossary.htm

Tour Check

- ○ Review guiding questions.
- ○ Stick to the tour itinerary.
- ○ Check off sites visited.
- ○ Skim and scan for needed data.
- ○ Keep notes as you go.
- ○ Record direct quotes you find useful with proper citations.
- ○ Make use of "hypertext links" within the website for further detail.
- ○ Use the "back" arrow to return to original site or look for a link to the "Home Page" if you get lost.
- ○ Revisit the guiding questions and continue touring until you have fulfilled your exploration.

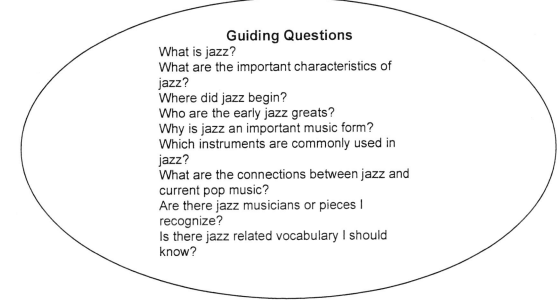

Guiding Questions
What is jazz?
What are the important characteristics of jazz?
Where did jazz begin?
Who are the early jazz greats?
Why is jazz an important music form?
Which instruments are commonly used in jazz?
What are the connections between jazz and current pop music?
Are there jazz musicians or pieces I recognize?
Is there jazz related vocabulary I should know?

Jazz E-tour Map

Where did jazz begin?

Who are the early jazz greats?

What are important characteristics of jazz?

Why is jazz an important music form?

Which instruments are commonly used in jazz?

What is jazz?

Jazz Jargon

What are the connections between jazz and current pop music?

Jazz musicians or pieces I recognize.

What next? (Potential topics or questions for further research.)

Sensemaking Model
Visualizing/Re-Conceptualizing

Sensemaking Model
Visualizing / Re-Conceptualizing

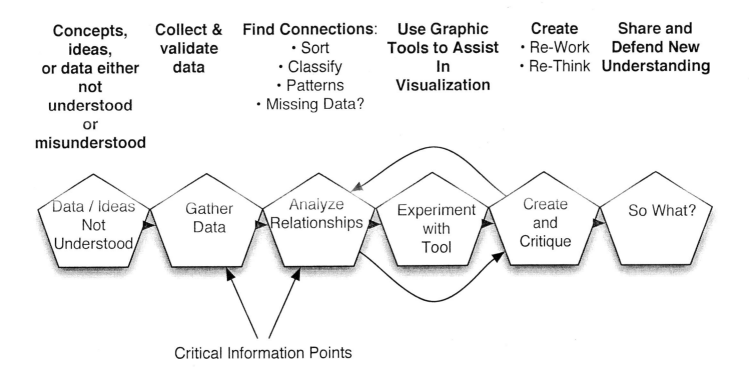

Concepts, ideas, or data either not understood or misunderstood

Collect & validate data

Find Connections:
- Sort
- Classify
- Patterns
- Missing Data?

Use Graphic Tools to Assist In Visualization

Create
- Re-Work
- Re-Think

Share and Defend New Understanding

Data / Ideas Not Understood · Gather Data · Analyze Relationships · Experiment with Tool · Create and Critique · So What?

Critical Information Points

Why Use This Model?

- Take advantage of the addage that a picture is worth a thousand words
- Take advantage of learners who have high visualization abilities
- Add one more dimension to text and explanations
- Use when data cannot be understood in their raw form
- Try several visualizations of the same ideas
- Particularly useful for concepts where misconceptions abound

Possible Topics:

- Popular misconceptions
- Data in any discipline
- Large amounts of data
- Population patterns
- All types of maps
- Ideas and their connections
- Cause / Effect
- Environmental / social issues
- Difficult concepts

Critical Information Literacy Skills*

- Evaluate Resources, K&Z p.34
- Use Organizers, K&Z p. 90
- Sort, K&Z p. 94
- Compare, K&Z p. 98
- Classify, K&Z p. 102

* Koechlin, Carol and Sandi Zwaan. *Build Your Own Information Literate School.* Hi Willow, 2003.

Notes on the Sensemaking Model

In an information-rich world, we naturally encounter a myriad of data, facts, and ideas that are meaningless unless they are organized. Examples include:

Data Encountered	Visualization for Sensemaking
• City names in alphabetical order	• Map
• A survey of opinions	• Results are graphed and charted
• Opinions at different times	• Graphic comparisons over time
• Weather data	• Map of a hurricane's position and likely path
• A list of organizational officers	• Organizational chart
• Data from a scientific instrument such as a seismograph or barometer	• Chart, graph, or map of results
• A list of elements	• The Periodic Table

We often misunderstand because we lack the ability to visualize. Consider the orbital path of our Moon. While some students may think it rises in the East and sets in the West, if charted properly, we discover the reverse to be true; the Moon actually rises in the West and sets in the East. The famous scientist Edward Tufte has made a career out of visualizing mass quantities of data to understand scientific, cultural, and technological phenomenon.[1] Yet even with simple concepts, students' right and left brains will benefit by both verbalizing and visualizing concepts and data.

Good teachers have used visualization as a tool as long as there have been teachers. In the vast world of new information, pictures serve to collapse vast quantities of data into an understandable form. Thus, we find teachers using many types of graphics such as mind maps, thinking maps, webs, clusters, network trees, fishbones, maps, graphic organizers, graphs, charts, tables, pictures, paintings, digital maps, and space photography to name but a few. The more data there are to digest and understand, the more effective sensemaking visualizations are. And the more students are involved in the creation of sensemaking visuals, the better they will be able to interpret not only their own creations but the creations of others. Since many questions on standardized tests require students to interpret various charts, tables, graphs, and other visuals, students who know how to construct and interpret visuals will do much better.

To teach sense-making, first ask students to collect data from an authoritative source. (Depending on their skill level, you may need to teach or review types of sources considered 'authoritative.') Then, allow them freedom to experiment with different visualization technology tools to create a picture of the data at hand. In

---

[1] Tufte, Edward. *The Visual Display of Quantitative Information.* Graphics Press, 2003.

their experiments with line graphs, for example, they may realize how the size of the interval selected affects the resulting picture. If they were to chart the national debt over the last five years using the interval billions of dollars the result would be an almost vertical line; however, if the interval were changed to trillions of dollars, the resulting graph would be an almost horizontal line. Students can have a great deal of fun producing different pictures of the same data, and then deciding which picture best expresses the data's meaning. In the budget example above, one political party might use the vertical chart, while another political party might use the horizontal chart to make their respective points.

Technology

The teaching process is twofold: instructing students in effective data gathering methods, and introducing them to various sense-making tools and technologies. These will range from simple pencil and paper to powerful computer programs able to analyze massive amounts of data.

Specific technologies to provide include:
- Concept-mapping software such as Inspiration
- Charting/graphing and numerical calculation software such as Microsoft Excel and numerous scientific calculators
- Map-making software such as Mapedit
- Timeline software such as Tom Snyder's TimeLiner
- Video editing software such as iMovie
- Flow charting software such as Omnigraffle

Research

In the book *Brain Matter: Translating Research Into Classroom Practice* by Patricia Wolfe[2], we are reminded that although each of us has the ability to process kinesthetic and auditory information, we take in more information visually than through any other senses and this capacity is almost unlimited.

Marzano[3] cites the use of non-linguistic representations as a powerful teaching technique that is well supported by research. For a review of this research, see his chapter six titled " Nonlinguistic Representations" pages 72-83

"The use of student and teacher-generated concept maps for teaching science concepts results in improved student achievement and positive student attitudes."[4]

---

[2] Wolfe, Patricia. *Brain Matters: Translating Research into Classroom Practice.* Alexandria VA: Association Supervision and Curriculum Development, 2001.

[3] Marzano, Robert J., Debra J. Pickering, and Jane E. Pollock. *Classroom Instruction that Works: Research-Based Strategies for Increasing Student Achievement.* ASCD, 2004.

[4] Cawelti, Gordon, ed. *Handbook of Research on Improving Student Achievement.* 3rd ed. Educational Research Service, 2004, p. 208.

Critical Information Skills for Sensemaking Model

Evaluate Resources
Students will evaluate resources for usefulness.

Determining whether or not resources are useful and reliable sources of information is a critical step when dealing with volumes of data. Students must first develop an awareness of their information need and then scan the text for evidence of relevance. They must also learn how to validate a resource by checking the contents against determined criteria. They need to realize that not everything they read, hear, and view, is reliable. The fact that it is produced in some way doesn't necessarily make it accurate or reliable. Students need strategies for examining information sources critically and lots and lots of practice applying them.

Use Organizers
Students will use graphic organizers to help analyze and synthesize data.

Graphic organizers are very useful processing tools. Like any other tools students need to be taught how to use them. Then they need to be given the support to adapt, modify and ultimately create their own. Using graphic organizers helps students to break data apart and analyze it. Similarly strategically designed templates can help students to work with data and build personal meaning. All templates need to be modeled in familiar contexts and applied repeatedly so students learn how and when to use each.

Sort
Students will sort gathered data for specific purposes

Sorting is an important entry-level analysis skill. Provide students with tactile/concrete sorting experiences before tackling the sorting of data. E.g. sort pictures, books, stamps, etc. Before students begin to sort, clear purpose and criteria must be established.

Compare
Students will make comparisons to discover relationships in gathered data.

Making comparisons is actually a complex process. Students must first of all determine exactly what is being compared and why, then decide which aspects of the items they will examine for the purposes of comparison. Consequently they need at least two bodies of information and pre-determined criteria to help sort the points of comparison. Once sorted, they need to determine what is similar and what is different.

Classify
Students will classify data gathered for specific purposes.

Classifying formalizes the sorting process by applying a system or principle. This high level activity is a very important skill that information users need to understand. All information sources (e.g. non-fiction books, specialized encyclopedias, newspapers, videos, Web Sites etc.) are structured or organized using a system or principle. Experiences with sorting and classifying data will help students to understand how to find information when they need it.

Examples of the Sensemaking Model

Unit 6: Chains and Webs   Gr. 4–7

What does a food chain look like? How do food chains form a food web in an ecosystem?

Problem: Students are studying the complex balance of ecosystems. Their problem is to create a visual representation of this complexity by creating the food chains and webs within the ecosystem they have studied.

Gather Data: Students need to plan their investigation, develop key words for searches and use a variety of reliable sources to gather data about life within their ecosystem.

Analyze Relationships: As students gather the names of plant and animal life that live in their ecosystem, they should begin to organize this information in charts or webs.
Students should look for relationships and develop flow charts of each food chain. They will examine the food chains for further links and build food webs within their ecosystem.

Select and Use Effective Tool: Demonstrate the use of effective software such as Inspiration™ for showing relationships and building webs.

Create and Critique: Students create their visual webs and confirm their inter-relationships by reviewing the notes and/or consulting their references. They peer review and revise as necessary to create the most effective visual representation of the food chains and webs within their ecosystem.

So What?
Next question: What happens if any component of the food chain is weakened or eliminated?
Read *Wolf Island* and *Ladybug Garden* by Cecilia Godkin to the students to help them begin thinking about broken food chains.

Unit 7: Population Patterns   Gr. 9–12

Discover population patterns and demonstrate visually.

Problem: Examine and analyze population statistics for patterns.

Gather Data: Ensure a cross representation of developed and developing countries and areas of the world are examined. Validate all sources of information. Decide on the categories of data to collect so they can be recorded in a spreadsheet or database for analysis (e.g. ages and gender of people, occupations, education, types of communities, span in years or decades).

Analyze Relationships: In small groups, have students examine the data collected and look for possible patterns, connections, missing, and conflicting data. Revisit sources as necessary to fill gaps. Have students use the potential of the spreadsheet software or database to experiment with relationships and visual representation (e.g. line graph, bar graph, pie chart, population pyramid, flow chart, and map). Groups study the results and develop some hypothesis statements about their findings.

Select and Use Effective Tool: Groups decide on the most effective visuals to provide a clear picture of their hypothesis.

Create and Critique: Groups plan their presentation and decide on a presentation format (e.g. overheads, slide show, pamphlet, poster, etc). Groups develop their presentation, rehearse, and share findings.

So What?
After group sharing, list and discuss common findings and discrepancies in understandings. Discuss how multiple interpretations of the same data could occur. What are the implications?

Unit 8: *Stella Louella's Runaway Book*   Gr. 2–4

How did Stella Louella's library book get lost? How can we find it?

Problem: What clues help the reader discover the title of the book that Louella lost?

Gather Data: Read and enjoy the story *Stella Louella's Runaway Book*. Have students meet in small groups to re-read the story and record the names of the characters on index cards. As the story progresses, ask them to use the other side of the card to record a clue offered by that character.

Analyze Relationships: Ask each group to read *Goldilocks and the Three Bears*. Have students develop index cards (use a different color) for the characters in this traditional story and cards for each major event. Ask students to look for relationships between the characters and events of *Goldilocks and the Three Bears* and the clues in *Stella Louella's Runaway Book*.

Select and Use Effective Tool: Model for students how effective a T-chart is for comparing things such as a tree and a flower.

Create and Critique: Have each group sort the index cards onto a T-chart comparing the two stories. Instruct them to join clues and events with colored string to create a chart that shows the relationships between the clues in *Stella Louella's Runaway Book* and the characters and events in *Goldilocks and the Three Bears.*

So What?

Share other stories with students dependent on clues such as *The Jolly Postman*. Have small groups of students develop a set of clues for well-known stories or fairy tales. Share with other groups and try to guess the story.

Suggested Picture Books for this Task

Ernst Campbell, Lisa. *Stella Louella's Runaway Book*. NY: Simon and Schuster Children's Publishing Division, 2001.

Ahlberg, Janet. *Each Peach Pear Plum*. Boston: Little, Brown and Company, 1991.

Ahlberg, Allan and Ahlberg Janet. *The Jolly Postman*. Boston: Little, Brown and Company, 1986.

Ahlberg, Allan and Ahlberg Janet. *The Jolly Christmas Postman*. Boston: Little, Brown and Company, 1991.

Ahlberg, Allan and Ahlberg Janet. *The Jolly Pocket Postman*. Boston: Little, Brown and Company, 1995.

Ernst Campbell, Lisa. *Stella Louella's Runaway Book*. New York: Simon and Schuster Children's Publishing Division, 2001.

Unit 9: Zebra Mussels   Gr. 5–8

What impact do zebra mussels have on humans and the environment?

Problem/Issue:
Students are examining the impact that the introduction of a foreign organism has on an ecosystem. Model collaboratively using the zebra mussel invasion.

Gather Data:
Show a video clip that highlights the zebra mussel invasion of the Great Lakes system in North America. Invite students to share their personal knowledge about the rapid spread of zebra mussels. Ask students to identify key stakeholders affected by zebra mussels. What was affected? How? What are the implications?

Analyze Relationships
Provide students with the blank organizer *Discovering Impact*. Explain the terms on the chart with examples from the video. Collaboratively start filling in the chart with data gleaned from the video and student personal knowledge. Have students work on selected Internet sites to discover more information on the zebra mussel invasion. Share findings to complete the chart. (See completed Teacher Resource sheet *Discovering Impact*.)

Experimenting with Tool
Introduce other examples of human intervention that impact an ecosystem (e.g. mustard seed on the prairies, reintroduction of wolves in the West, forest clear cutting, genetically modified crops). Ask students to conduct a similar investigation to discover who or what was affected, how and what the implications are. Stress the importance of identifying all of key stakeholders. Review a variety of typical organizers. See *Go Graphic*. Instruct students to use the organizer provided or design one of their own that will help them make connections and demonstrate impact.

Create and Critique
Provide students with *Graphic Organizer Check* so they can self and/or peer assess completed organizers.

So What?
Students start to build a file of graphic organizers to select from or adapt for each new task.

Gathering Evidence of Understanding
- data gathered is accurate, adequate and relevant
- students sorted data and recorded it in appropriate sections of organizer
- students discovered implications and came to a personal conclusion
- checklists were used to assess and improve completed organizers

InfoSkills
- evaluate resources
- use organizers, design an organizer
- understand perspective, identify and consider
- use organizers
- impact, examine effects, examine perspectives, evaluate effects

Reflect, Rethink, Redesign
- Were students able to identify key stakeholders? If not how can we locate additional resources that include a larger variety of stakeholders?
- Did students find the organizer helpful as collected their data? Which students had difficulty? How could I help them?
- Do they understand how organizers are designed to help them make connections? Should I provide more opportunities for them to use specific types of organizers?
- Where else in the curriculum would organizers be of benefit for students?
- Are there students who are ready to create their own organizers? Can I arrange for them to use computer software to create custom organizers?
- Should I provide some prompts to help them make the connections between affects and the implications of those affects?

Determining Impact

Topic: Zebra Mussels in the Great Lakes

Who/what was affected?	How?	What are the implications?
Boats - navigational and recreational	- mussels attach to hull and engine parts	- increased drag from weight - overheating of engine - damage to cooling system
Fishing gear	- fouled if left in the water too long	- damaged beyond repair - expensive to replace
Navigation buoys and docks	- mussels attach and weight them down	- encrusted and sink - corrosion of steel - weakening of concrete
Beaches	- broken shells and foul smell	- ruins appearance - danger to bare feet
Native mussels	- attacked by zebra mussels - latch on to them	- interferes with feeding, growth, movement and respiration, as well as reproduction - clams cannot open shells
Water supply pipes of hydroelectric and nuclear power plants Public water supplies Industrial facilities	- mussels attach and constrict flow	- reduced water intake and flow - damages fore fighting equipment - damages air conditioning and cooling systems - damages irrigation systems
Cottagers	- constant battle to keep lakes clean	- clogged water systems expensive to repair - damage to docks, boats and fishing gear - sharp shells are dangerous - need to rinse boats all the time
Whitefish, sculpin, smelt, and chubb	- starving because they cannot find Diporeia, tiny shrimp-like crustaceans. - Diporeia loss is due to competition for algae with the zebra mussels	-loss to commercial fishing of whitefish and also trout and salmon which because the smaller fish are prey for them
Clarity of water	- mussels filter algae from the water turning it clear	- increased scuba diving on the great lakes now - increase in aquatic plants provides cover and nurseries for some new species of fish

In view of this information…

This invasion is a disaster for the great Lakes water system. The damage to the environment and industry is growing daily. The methods that have been tried to rid the lake of these pests have not been successful.
Are boaters doing all they can to stop the spread of zebra mussels? Are people taking this problem seriously?
Surely scientists can do something before it is too late? What if the problem is never solved? We can't let zebra mussels spread to all the fresh water in North America.
Why can't a natural predator be introduced? Could a control area be set up to experiment with some natural solutions?

Sample completion of **Determing Impact**, *InfoTasks for Successful Learning*, Pembroke Publishers

Discovering Impact

Topic:..

Who/what was affected?	How?	What are the implications?

In view of this information...

GO Graphic

Graphic organizers are useful visual tools to help you process the data you have gathered.

Use them to build personal meaning:
- ❑ **sort** facts into categories or sub-topics
- ❑ display a **sequence** of events or procedures
- ❑ **compare** and contrast information
- ❑ identify **connect**ing ideas
- ❑ **distinguish** between fact and opinion
- ❑ **analyze** conflicting information
- ❑ **identify** bias and perspective
- ❑ **identify** cause and effect
- ❑ **determine** relationships

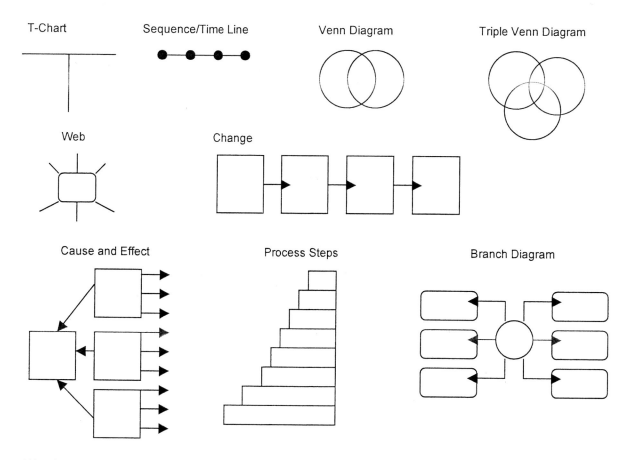

T-Chart   Sequence/Time Line   Venn Diagram   Triple Venn Diagram

Web   Change

Cause and Effect   Process Steps   Branch Diagram

Why do you need an organizer? You can ask your teachers for ready-made templates or you can create your own on the computer using draw software. Make use of shapes, arrows, shading and color. Try out some ideas and make sketches of your own design. **Which organizer is best for your need? Why?**

Adapted from *Student Research Guide*, Toronto District School Board

Graphic Organizer Check ☑

Use this checklist to help you think about the kind of organizer you need and later to check if you have applied all the design elements of this visual tool.

See *Go Graphic* for some basic organizers to get you started.

Use graphic organizers to:
- ☐ sort facts into categories
- ☐ compare and contrast information
- ☐ classify information
- ☐ distinguish between fact and fiction
- ☐ determine relationships
- ☐ display a sequence of events
- ☐ display connecting ideas
- ☐ identify cause and effect
- ☐ draw conclusions
- ☐ make a web or mind map
- ☐ organize ideas
- ☐ plan for writing
- ☐ make a decision
- ☐ solve a problem
- ☐ other

You can:
- ☐ use a teacher-made organizer
- ☐ find one on the Internet
- ☐ adapt a ready made organizer
- ☐ create your own organizer by hand
- ☐ create your own organizer using word processing draw tools
- ☐ use specialized software to create your own organizer

Some design and content elements to check:
- ☐ correct spelling and grammar
- ☐ factual data backed up with an accurate reference list
- ☐ visual design aids understanding
- ☐ neat and attractive
- ☐ use of arrows, shading and color to add to clarity
- ☐ appropriate font and style to aid readability
- ☐ a title and your name or group names

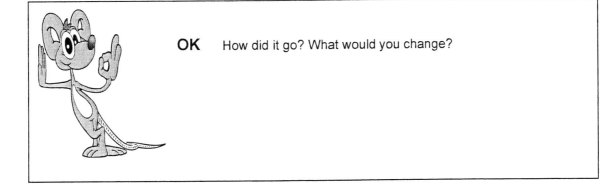

OK   How did it go? What would you change?

The Read, View, Listen Model

The Read, View, Listen Model

Introduce the topic(s) to be explored along with Objectives

Groups or individuals read, view or listen to many or several items on topic

Compare/ contrast items on theme elements

Summary/ synthesis Activity

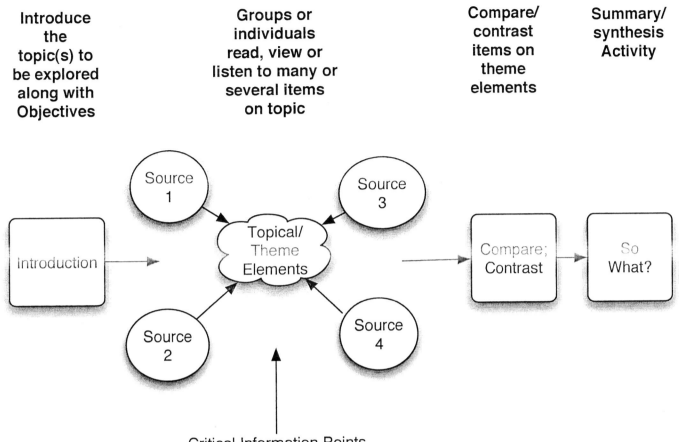

Critical Information Points

Why Use This Model?

• Experience many literary/ written works rather than a single text
• Allow all skill levels to concentrate on the theme rather than the difficulty of the text
• Concept map the big ideas across texts
• See big picture across cultures, authors, governments, time periods, ideas
• When you can't afford a textbook but have a library

Possible Topics:

• Literary themes across books
• Similar literary themes across cultures
• Causes of wars across combatants
• News reporting across international newspapers & TV
• Teen angst across teen novels
• Comparison of cultures around the world at the same time period
• Lives of rich and poor - same time, same locale

Critical Information Literacy Skills*

• Pre-Reading Strategies, K&Z p. 52
• Skim, Scan, and Consider, K&Z p. 32
• Actively Read, View and Listen, K&Z p. 56
• Read Pictures, K&Z p. 70
• Compare, K&Z p. 98

*Koechlin, Carol and Sandi Zwaan. *Build Your Own Information Literate school*. Hi Willow, 2003

Notes on the Read, View, Listen Model

Most of us have been used to students in a class reading the same textbook chapter, the same novel, the same poem, or the same directions for a chemical experiment. The reading is assigned and homework expected without considering or supporting students' variable abilities. In fact, a majority of the students in many North American classrooms, if left unaided, cannot read the assigned texts with the necessary comprehension. To ignore this issue establishes a knowledge barrier between us and our students; we fail them if we do not provide the additional/alternative resources necessary for them to succeed.

The more diverse the abilities, cultural backgrounds, or the socioeconomic conditions of our students, the more essential a large library collection becomes to ensure successful differentiation. In fact, one could say the library is the *only* hope for many students trying to accomplish what teachers are asking. The Read, View, Listen Model assumes that an information-rich environment can supply many materials on almost any issue or topic.

Using this model, the teacher and librarian collaborate to first choose a state standard and a topic embraced by that standard. Themes abound in all disciplines: good vs. evil, moral vs. immoral, justice vs. injustice, or love vs. hate. Rather than assigning a single text for the exploration of this theme, the teacher and librarian provide a wide variety of materials with which students can engage. By meeting students at their own level and involving their varying interests, each learner will develop a deep understanding of the central concept. For example, the Cinderella story is common in many cultures, and its versions range from very easy to read, to full-length novel, to Hollywood motion picture, to picture book. Depending on their ability and cultural background, students can sample a wide variety of materials in various formats to achieve the goal.

One thinks of enriching the study of *Romeo and Juliet, The Merchant of Venice, Othello,* or *Hamlet* with a plethora of materials ranging from classics, to illustrated comic books, from Lamb's retelling of the plays, to popular Hollywood films from the early 20th century to the present, from annotated or illustrated editions of the plays in print, to computer programs that automatically define or provide definitions if the mouse is passed across any word. The list inspires, but the variety it offers is impossible in an information-poor environment.

Yet how does one control the progress through a theme, you might ask, when everyone in the class is reading, viewing, or listening to something different? Using skimming and scanning techniques, or fostering good questions, fascinating discussions, or complimentary projects would allow the teacher and librarian to mark progress along the way while students are actually enjoying the rich garden of learning materials. Many teachers have discovered that using a wide variety of materials on a single theme can be used as a prelude to the understanding of a difficult, original text.

In other disciplines such as the social sciences, the theme of justice vs. injustice is served when students are reading a wide variety of materials on the topic. Suddenly, they may realize that race relations not common in their own country are commonplace in other cultures. And even when skin color is not an issue, cultures find ways to discriminate, such as by height in the famous Hutu vs. Tutsi conflict.

Teachers who are accustomed to using a single text may experience frustration and failure as their students seem to wander through multiple text or works, but with a little practice, their expectations for understanding and achievement can become very high, and results improved immeasurably.

Two common examples of tweak in normal learning experiences would be the Great Books Program and Literature Circles. In both of these programs, the emphasis is usually on the study of a single text. However, if multiple texts are substituted with a similar theme, many of the tried and true techniques of these programs still work and can be amplified.

Technology

The technology used will correlate with the various genres and formats for materials available on any topic. Playback technologies such as CD players, video equipment (VHS and/or DVD), streaming Internet audio/video, plus the print technologies such as hardback books, paperback books, and comic books will draw a reader.

Research

In his book *Building Background Knowledge for Academic Achievement* (ASCD, 2004), Robert Marzano encourages wide reading, particularly in SSR programs as supportable by numerous research studies. See his chapter three: "Tapping the Power of Wide Reading and Language Experience."

Stephen Krashen's *The Power of Reading: Insights From the Research*, 2nd edition (Libraries Unlimited, 2004) documents the power that wide reading, particularly free voluntary reading as a powerful predictor of skill in comprehension, writing style, grammar, spelling, and vocabulary.

"Extensive reading of material of many kinds both in school and outside results in substantial growth in vocabulary and comprehension abilities and in the information base of students." Gordon Cawelty, ed. *Handbook of Research on Improving student Achievement*. 3rd ed. (Educational Research service, 2004)

Critical Information Skills for Read, View, Listen Model

Pre-reading Strategies
Students will develop pre-reading strategies for non-fiction.

These strategies will provide some background knowledge, and help students make connections between what they already know and the new content. Pre-reading strategies also help students predict what the text will be about. To be successful readers of non-fiction text, students must be able to establish a purpose for reading. All strategies need to be modeled and practiced many times.

Skim, Scan, Consider
Students will skim and scan resources to discover which information is relevant to their information need.

Skim and scan are old information skills that have not only stood the test of time but have become increasingly more important as the volume of data available explodes. This set of pre reading skills is a vital prerequisite for using information texts. When these skills are taught and practiced in relevant and purposeful experiences they will have more meaning for students. Skim, scan, and consider must become a natural pre-reading strategy for all information tasks.

Actively Read, View, Listen
Students will actively and productively read, view, and listen to a variety of resources to extract information relevant to their need.

Today's multimedia world provides a bombardment of fast paced, non-linear information bytes. The implications of the new literacies for the 21st century require us to ensure that all students can decode or "read" all formats including non-written texts. We must teach students how to interact with all types of media text. They must be able to actively read, view, listen, hunt for key ideas, develop questions, make connections, and reflect on their discoveries. Students need to be not only active but also critical users of information sources.

Read Pictures
Students will decode information from video, pictures in books, and photographs in newspapers and magazines, to discover implicit and explicit information messages they contain.

Illustrations and photographs in both fiction and non-fiction texts hold a wealth of information. While some information is very obvious, much of the information must be uncovered. Students need experiences decoding this kind of visual information, as well as opportunities and practice in analyzing it. This skill will prepare students for broader visual literacy skills. Visual skills are critical to information processing today since so much of the information students access is loaded with powerful images. Critical reading of visual images is necessary to uncover all the intended information.

Compare
Students will make comparisons to discover relationships in gathered data.

Making comparisons is actually a complex process. Students must first of all determine exactly what is being compared and why, then decide which aspects of the items they will examine for the purposes of comparison. Consequently they need at least two bodies of information and pre-determined criteria to help sort the points of comparison. Once sorted, they need to determine what is similar and what is different.

Examples of the Read, View, Listen Model

Unit 10: Questions, Questions   Gr. 2–3

How do my questions help me when I read?

Introduce
With riddles, review the question starters who, what, when, where, why and how. Select an engaging picture book related to your topic of study. Look at the cover and have students ask questions about the cover. Chart the questions highlighting the question starters. Read a few pages and have students make up more questions. Continue charting and questioning until the book is completed. Ask students: Are there any questions that we now have the answers to? How could we find answers to some of your other questions? How have questions helped us to enjoy the story more?

Read, View, Listen
In small groups of three or four, provide students with either a text for read aloud sharing, or multiple texts on the same topic for independent reading. This strategy works well with both fiction and non-fiction texts. Have students practice the strategy using the *Question, Question* organizer. They write down their questions before reading, during reading, and after reading the text. Have students circle or highlight the question starters they have used. Remind them to make use of all the question starters if they can.

Compare/Contrast
Ask students to review their questions and cross off all the ones they now have answers to. Share in their group and see if anyone else has the same or similar questions about the topic. They could use a coding system to mark questions already answered, similar questions, and different or unique questions.

So What?
Students could identify a question or several questions they are really curious about and begin a new quest to discover the answers.

Unit 11: Magical Rainforests   Gr. 4–6

Why should we be concerned about rainforest ecosystems?

Introduction
Read aloud *The Great Kapok Tree* by Lynne Cherry. Help students begin to make connections to the issues by using the following prompts exercise. When in the story did you feel content, happy, worried, sad, or anxious? Introduce the guiding question.

Read, View Listen
Provide students with the organizer *RVL Connect*. Explain the organizer and model by asking for responses based on the reading of *The Great Kapok Tree*. Introduce an educational video that you have previewed about the sustainability of rainforests. Select the best video no more than 30 minutes in length. Chunk the viewing in 5-10 minute segments if possible. Show the video, stop and ask students to record responses, and continue to view and respond until the video is completed.

Compare
Assemble students in groups of four to share their findings and responses. Ask them to identify common understandings, concerns, and questions. Debrief with the entire class and focus on the guiding question. Chart collective responses.

So What?
Students could select a question or concern of interest for further study or investigate taking action to protect a particular rainforest.

Unit 12: Where's the Beef?   Gr. 9–12

What are the potential effects of Mad Cow Disease on local, national and global economies?

Introduction

Economics classes are investigating international reactions to examples of crisis situations in major market products. The first crisis topic is Mad Cow Disease, known formally as bovine spongiform encephalopathy or BSE. Introduce by showing students some political cartoons on the topic and discussing the perspectives and issues represented. Ask students what they know about this topic and chart their responses. Identify the main countries of concern and the possible perspectives that should be investigated.

Read View Listen

Form groups and ask the students to divide up the work so that major countries and stakeholders involved will be investigated. Have students conduct searches in periodical databases that subscribe to international papers. Each student should select at least three articles to review. Provide students with copies of the *Concept Mapping Worksheet* so they can record their notes and create concept maps from the information gleaned in each article.

Compare

Instruct students in the groups to share their summary notes and concept maps. Review the guiding question. Have the group create a chart to record the potential effects of Mad Cow Disease on local, national and global economies that they have researched. Instruct students to identify their sources, the perspectives taken and any overt media spin on the issue.

Country	Occurrences	Effects	Potential Impact

Return to search more articles if necessary. Share and discuss common findings and discrepancies.

So What?

Students select another crisis topic and conduct an independent study following the class model.

Unit 13: Mosquito Alert　　Gr. 9–12

How well are we coping with the threat of West Nile Virus?

Introduction

Ask students to share what they already know about West Nile Virus. Chart this information. Read aloud a short current article about West Nile Virus. Discuss and chart new information. Highlight new terms and vocabulary. Introduce the guiding question. Inform students that they will work in InfoTeams: Data Digger, Wordsmith, Illustrator, Reflector, Questioner. They will explore a variety of sources to help them focus on this question. They will each have a specific role in their team and that role will rotate daily for five sessions. Introduce and model the roles (see *InfoTeamwork* organizers) by returning to the short article and sharing responses for each of the five role tasks.

Read, View, Listen

In groups students use selected current articles, books, videos, news clips, websites and data from science and health organizations selected to represent all relevant players and cross-country perspectives. Assign role schedules and provide copies of *InfoTeamwork* organizers (each team consisting of all five roles). Remind students to focus on the guiding question as they are researching and completing their role tasks. Allow two-thirds of class time for reading and completing role tasks and one-third for the sharing circle. Every day students take on a new role using a new resource. Give students time to review their role worksheets and to complete their *Learning Log for InfoTeamwork.*

Compare

Every day students share the information they discovered through their assigned role. The group then focuses on the guiding question looking for common understandings about the threat of West Nile Virus and the problems and successes of coping with it. As a class, discuss common findings and record on chart paper.

So What?

InfoTeams can now tackle another health topic of concern and apply their new skills (e.g. Mad Cow Disease, SARS...).

Gathering Evidence of Understanding

o teams collected and recorded relevant information accurately
o information from different roles complimented and supported the findings of others
o students completed their tasks in role
o students compared findings and discovered commonalities

Info Skills:

o pre-reading strategies
o skim, scan, and consider
o actively read, view and listen
o read pictures
o compare

Reflect, Rethink, Redesign:

o Were resources adequate?
o Were there resources to support all the student skill levels?
o Can I identify areas of student strengths and weaknesses as they try different roles?
o How can I help students cope in their areas of weakness?
o Are group discussions successful? Are there groups that need guidance?
o Was there evidence of contradictory information? How did students determine what was actual fact?
o Do students see the value of the variety in approaches to recording and understanding information?

Question, Question

I am reading..

by..

How do questions help me when I read?

Before Reading

During Reading

After Reading

☑ I know the answer now.	★ No one else has this question.
☺ Someone has the same question.	◎ I am really curious about this.

RVL Connect

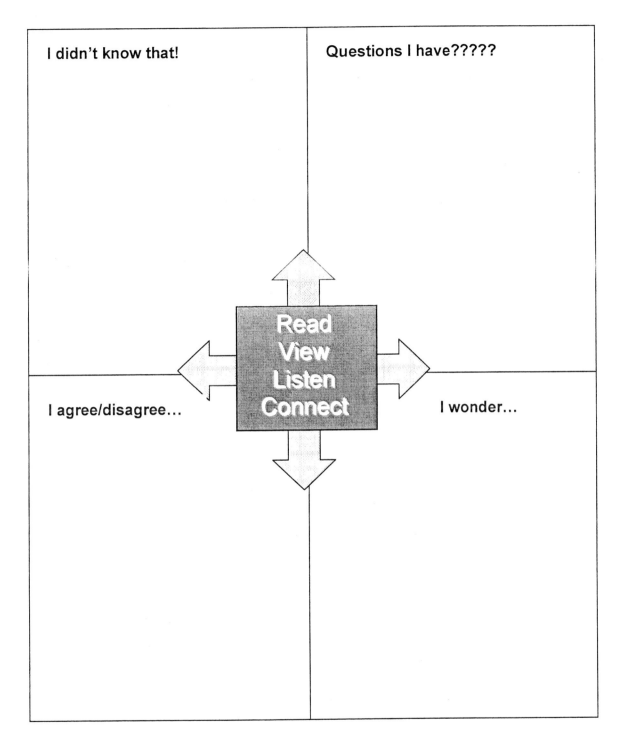

I didn't know that!

Questions I have?????

Read View Listen Connect

I agree/disagree…

I wonder…

Title of resource…………………………………………………………………………

Kind of resource…………………………………………………………………………

Concept Mapping Worksheet

Use the following worksheet to record notes as you read in the left hand column and make a concept map in the right hand column. Create your own form as you get experience.

Reading Log	
Source (Citation of what I am reading):	
My reading notes:	Concept map of ideas I am encountering:
Summary of what I have read:	

Learning Log for InfoTeamwork

Date……………………….................……Role……………………………………………...
Today's Source:………………………………………………………………………………………
Reflections:……………………………………………………………………………………………
………
………

Date……………………….................……Role……………………………………………...
Today's Source:………………………………………………………………………………………
Reflections:……………………………………………………………………………………………
………
………

Date……………………….................……Role……………………………………………...
Today's Source:………………………………………………………………………………………
Reflections:……………………………………………………………………………………………
………
………

Date……………………….................……Role……………………………………………...
Today's Source:………………………………………………………………………………………
Reflections:……………………………………………………………………………………………
………
………

Date……………………….................……Role……………………………………………...
Today's Source:………………………………………………………………………………………
Reflections:……………………………………………………………………………………………
………
………

Date:…………………………………..…
Summary thoughts and new questions:
………
………
………
………
………
………
………
………
………

InfoTeamwork

Name:..Team:...........................

Book:...

Reading for today is page.....................to page.....................

Illustrator: Your job is to read a section of your book and decide how you can share the information you have discovered using a visual interpretation. It can be a picture, cartoon, labeled sketch, graph, etc. Prepare to share with your team.

Adapted from *InfoTasks for Successful Learning*, Pembroke, 2001

InfoTeamwork

Name:..Team:...........................

Book:...

Reading for today is page....................to page....................

> **Today you are the Data Digger.**

Data Digger: Your job is to read a section of your book and find fascinating and significant bits of information. Jot down these gems on your organizer and record why this data is important. Prepare to share with your team.

Interesting Data	Why it is important

Adapted from *InfoTasks for Successful Learning*, Pembroke, 2001

Put a star beside the most exciting data. You want to make sure you share this with your group.

InfoTeamwork

Name:..Team:......................

Book:...

Reading for today is page....................to page...................

Questioner: Your job is to skim through your book, read pictures and graphics, headlines, sidebars and subtitles. As you are skimming, jot down questions you have about things you are discovering. Put a sticky note on the pages you have questions about so you can find them quickly when you are sharing with your team.

Who	
What	
When	
Where	
Why	
How	

Adapted from *InfoTasks for Successful Learning,* Pembroke, 2001

InfoTeamwork

Name:...Team:.........................

Book:...

Reading for today is page.....................to page.....................

Wordsmith: Your job is to read a section of your book. As you read be watching for new and interesting vocabulary. Record these words and phrases as well as what you think they mean. Use a dictionary to make sure you have the correct meaning. Plan to share your words with the team.

Interesting word/phrase	What it means

The word/phrase of the day is:

Why?

Adapted from *InfoTasks for Successful Learning*, Pembroke, 2001

InfoTeamwork

Name:...Team:.................

Today you are the Reflector.

Book:...

Reading for today is page.................to page...................

Reflector: Read a section in your book. Use the reflection prompts on your organizer to help you make connections to your new discoveries. Prepare to share with your team.

A main point I discovered: ....

....

I can use this information...

....

I was surprised to find out that...

..................because...

I didn't know that...

....

I think that..

because...

The most important thing to remember is...

....

I wonder if...

....

Adapted from *InfoTasks for Successful Learning*, Pembroke, 2001

Advice to Action Model

Advice to Action Model

An engaging problem or issue needing expert advice	Predict / guestimate possible advice from experts	Build background of the issue	Gather, sort, and analyze expert witnesses and advice	Test ideas with others; Compare to value system	Decide on a course of action

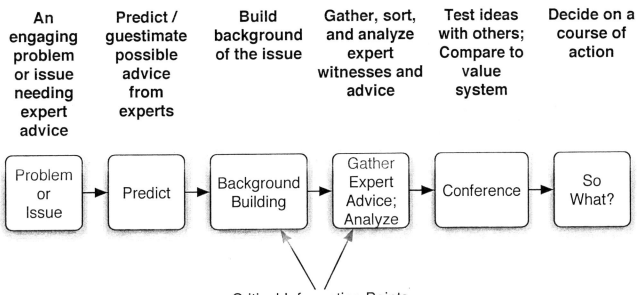

Problem or Issue → Predict → Background Building → Gather Expert Advice; Analyze → Conference → So What?

Critical Information Points

Why This Model?

- To solve real problems
- Judge between good and poor advice
- Affect behavior: judging the difference between personal wishes and prudence
- Understanding the consequences of taking advice
- To understand how historical events were shaped by advice both good and poor
- Making life-saving decisions

Possible Topics:

- Healthy lifestyles
- Selecting a college or career
- Succeeding in school
- Preventing, controlling forest fires
- Urban sprawl
- Safe drinking water Vending machines in schools
- School fundraising initiatives
- School safety issues
- Helping the homeless

Critical Information Literacy Skills:

- Use Primary Sources, K&Z p. 46
- Evaluate Resources, K&Z p. 34
- Interpret, Infer, Predict, K&Z p. 130
- Understanding Perspective, K&Z p. 136
- Cause and Effect, K&Z p. 120

* Koechlin, Carol and Sandi Zwaan. *Build Your Own Information Literate School*. Hi Willow, 2003

Notes on the Advice to Action Model

Advice is cheap and plentiful. "Try this marijuana cigarette, everyone else is doing it." "Don't use condoms. They cause AIDS" (a common misconception in Africa). "Don't sail west because you will fall off the earth" (a common misconception in 15th century Europe). In an information-rich environment, students of all ages need to learn the power of discerning the quality of the advice they are given, whether it be advice on taking a behavioral action or advice on solving a problem. This teaching model asks students to abandon whim as a technique for taking action; rather, it asks them to seek the best advice upon which effective action can be based. The opportunities to teach this skill abound across all disciplines and across all grade levels. Examples include:

- How do we really help a homeless person?
- How do we say no to drugs?
- How do we choose our friends?
- What would be the best community service project I could do?
- Who should I support as a candidate for mayor?
- What is the West Nile Virus and how can I avoid contracting it?
- Will drinking Coca Cola get me a girlfriend/boyfriend?
- Will eating Cheerios prevent me from getting heart disease?

The dilemma, of course, is the one faced by Robert Frost in his poem, "The Road Not Taken," when he said:

> Two roads diverged in a narrow wood,
> ....
> I took the one less traveled by,
> And that has made all the difference.

Students soon learn that even authoritative advice may not be the best in the long run. We may go to war with Iraq based on the best advice available, or we may decide not to sail west from Spain; we may fail to post the 95 theses on the church door in Wittenberg, or sign the Declaration of Independence.

In using this technique, teachers and librarians help students confront an issue or problem by searching for and sorting information. Students will be asked to sort based on authoritative and believable advice and then build a case using logic and reason to support an action.

Technology

Advice, of course, can be sought from authoritative print sources: trusted online databases, websites, or experts from across the world. Students will need to be taught the techniques of using technology to find, sort, and evaluate such advice, and to chart or graph that advice on various continuums in order to make an analysis. Finally, they will need to synthesize in order to determine a wise course of action based on their findings. Teleconferencing to experts, video chats, email, and other interactive technologies will allow students to get advice and question that advice in real time.

Critical Information Skills for Advice to Action Model

Use Primary Sources
Students will collect and analyze primary sources of information

Sometimes the best source of information for a research topic is a primary source. When students are required to conduct an interview or a survey, they are gathering original primary data. When students analyze photographs or artifacts from a time period they are also working with first hand information. Historical primary sources can make the past come alive for students. To optimize these resources students need to learn how to interpret and analyze them. Technology has made it possible to bring many primary artifacts into the classroom virtually.

Evaluate Resources
Students will evaluate resources for usefulness.

Determining whether or not resources are useful and reliable sources of information is a critical step when dealing with volumes of data. Students must first develop an awareness of their information need and then scan the text for evidence of relevance. They must also learn how to validate a resource by checking the contents against determined criteria. They need to realize that not everything they read, hear, and view, is reliable. The fact that it is produced in some way doesn't necessarily make it accurate or reliable. Students need strategies for examining information sources critically and lots and lots of practice applying them.

Interpret, Infer, Predict
Students will interpret information to develop inferences and make predictions.

Analysis of data in the research process requires that students can take information they have gathered about their topic, examine it closely and develop personal understanding. They accomplish this by mentally and physically processing the gathered data. Students need to; interpret the meaning of the texts they are reading, viewing or listening to; make some inferences about the data based on text clues and prior knowledge and experiences; then apply their interpretation and inferences to making a personal prediction.

Understanding Perspective
Students will analyze information to identify and examine perspective in order to gain understanding.

Perspective is powerful when it comes to information. The ability to examine a text and determine perspective is an important skill for working with complex issues. To be able to gain understanding through perspective requires a high level of critical thinking. Helping students gain perspective empowers them to be alert and to keep a critical distance from accepted or common theories.

Cause & Effect
Students will work with information to determine cause and effect, relationships.

Cause tells why something happens and effect tells what happens. Effects are pretty easy to pin down however determining causal relationships is much trickier because cause involves digging back into the past. One of the challenges with this skill is avoiding the effect of emotions and prior learning experiences. They can sway our thinking so that and we jump to incorrect conclusions about causes of an event. Likewise interpretation of the effect is subject to perspective.

Examples of the Advice to Action Model

Unit 14: Safe Water   Gr. 5–6

How safe is the drinking water in our community?

Problem/Issue: Students are concerned about the quality of drinking water in their community.
Prediction: Small groups of students meet to discuss and record what they know about the water in their local community and then generate questions they will need to guide their investigation. What do they need to find out? Who can they ask? Where can they locate information about the quality of their drinking water? What can they expect to discover from their research?
Background: Students explore a variety of local and regional documents and periodical articles related to quality dinking water.
Expert Advice: Refine investigation questions and consult real experts in the field (e.g. Public Utilities, Health Organizations, Politicians, and Environmental experts. Analyze data in groups using a *That's Good That's Bad* organizer.
Conference: Groups share their analysis. Listen, question, discuss.
So What? Each student completes a *Forming Opinion* organizer and writes a letter to the local authorities stating their opinion—supported by facts—and their concerns about the quality of water in their community now and in the future.
Note: A video that would be a useful model for this task is *Making a difference with information: You Know It Series* produced by General Division Learning in association with American Association of School Librarians.

Unit 15: Resume Writing   Gr. 7–12

What are the elements of an effective resume?

Problem/Issue: Students need to develop the skills to create effective resumes to help in their search for summer employment.
Prediction: Groups of students brainstorm for possible content, format and style of effective resumes.
Building Background: Students individually search career ads in newspapers, job centers and websites. They use highlighters to identify information required for specific jobs. Re-group and share findings. Discuss and add any new ideas.
Expert Advice: Individually consult experts: job agencies, employers, parents, and websites. Gather samples. Return to groups with expert advice and sample resumes. Share and compile results. Have each group set up a display of their findings.
Conference: Students rotate through groups, listen to best advice, discuss, and question.
So What?
Each student develops their own checklist for writing an effective resume and then creates their own personal resume. Instruct them to critique with a friend, revise and edit. Remind students that each job they apply for will require tweaking of their resume so that it is customized to reflect the job requirements. They also will need to continuously keep updating their resume to include new experiences and skills as they acquire them.

Unit 16: Healthy Lifestyles   Gr. 8–12

How can teens make informed decisions about leading a healthy lifestyle?

Problem/Issue
In an integrated unit, students are studying healthy lifestyles and reading novels dealing with adolescent issues (e.g. drinking, smoking, AIDS, teen pregnancy, violence, sexual abuse, and performance-enhancing drugs).

Prediction
Ask students to identify the protagonist and the social or health issues they are dealing with in the novel they are reading. Record these on sticky notes and then cluster similar issues. Develop categories for these problems. Group students according to issue/problem and have each group brainstorm for possible causes and effects of their issue. Use *Investigating Social and Health Issues* to record ideas.

Background Building Group members research the issue from a variety of resources available in the school library. Review "evaluating resources." Take notes regarding the possible causes, effects and solutions for dealing with these adolescent problems.

Expert Individually, students consult experts (e.g. social workers, physicians, police, agencies, and guidance counselors). Complete the last section of the organizer. Share new information and discuss causes, effects and solutions in small groups.

Consultation Use the inner circle outer circle strategy; inner circle are the consultants, outer circle ask questions. Outer Circle moves clockwise three spaces and continues consultation with a new expert. Switch roles and continue consulting process.

So What?
Each student writes a letter to the protagonist in their novel with their best advice based on their discoveries during this learning process.

Gathering Evidence of Understanding
- problems and issues were identified accurately
- problems and issues were sorted appropriately
- research gleaned adequate and accurate background information
- students questioned and responded effectively in role
- letters were on topic and realistic

Info Skills:
- use primary sources
- evaluate resources
- interpret, infer, predict
- sort
- make connections
- cause & effect

Reflect, Rethink, Redesign
- Do all students have a novel appropriate for their own reading level?
- Was there meaningful discussion as students decided on categories?
- Are students making personal connections to events or problems in the novels they are reading?
- Is there any indication that individual students are disturbed by discussions about certain problems?
- Should I further involve the guidance staff? How?
- Did they understand the process for inner circle outer circle? Were they able to participate in role?
- What could I do to help those who couldn't?

Forming an Opinion

Use this organizer to help you draw **conclusions**.

Inquiry Question/Problem

My Ideas	Supporting Data

Have I examined all relevant points of view? Can I identify patterns and trends? Based on this evidence, what conclusions can I draw?

What do I believe is important? Why? How can I share my opinion with others?

Adapted from *InfoTasks for Successful Learning*, Pembroke Publishers

That's Good ⟺ That's Bad

That's Good	Why?		That's Bad	Why?
My analysis				

Adapted from Koechlin and Zwaan, *Info Tasks for Learning*, Pembroke Publishers 2001

Investigating Social and Health Issues

This organizer will help you make connections between events, their causes, and their consequences. Usually we notice the event first and then have to think backwards to determine what caused it, so fill in the events as you discover them and then use the connector words as clues to uncover the causes and effects of the events.

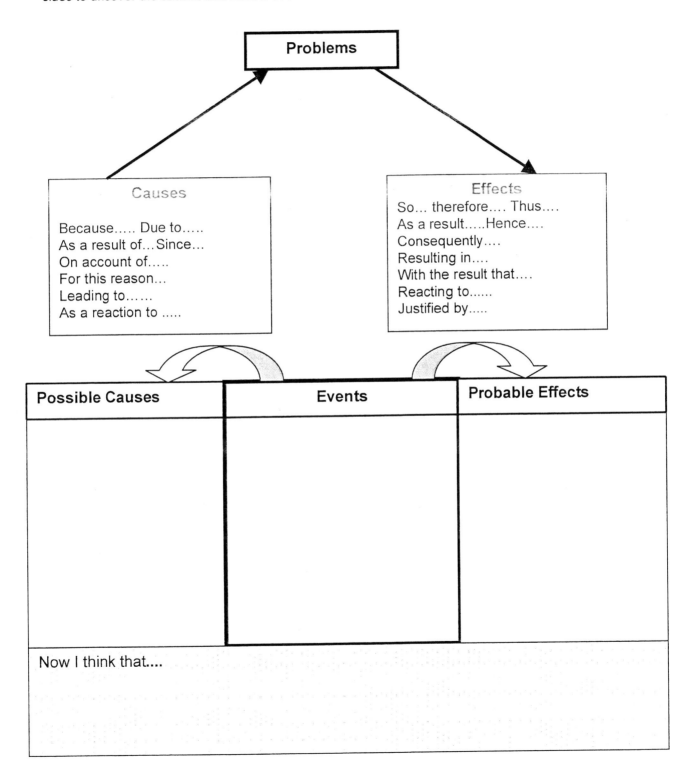

Problems

Causes

Because..... Due to.....
As a result of...Since...
On account of.....
For this reason...
Leading to......
As a reaction to .....

Effects

So... therefore.... Thus....
As a result.....Hence....
Consequently....
Resulting in....
With the result that....
Reacting to......
Justified by.....

Possible Causes	Events	Probable Effects

Now I think that....

Compare and Contrast Model

Compare and Contrast Model

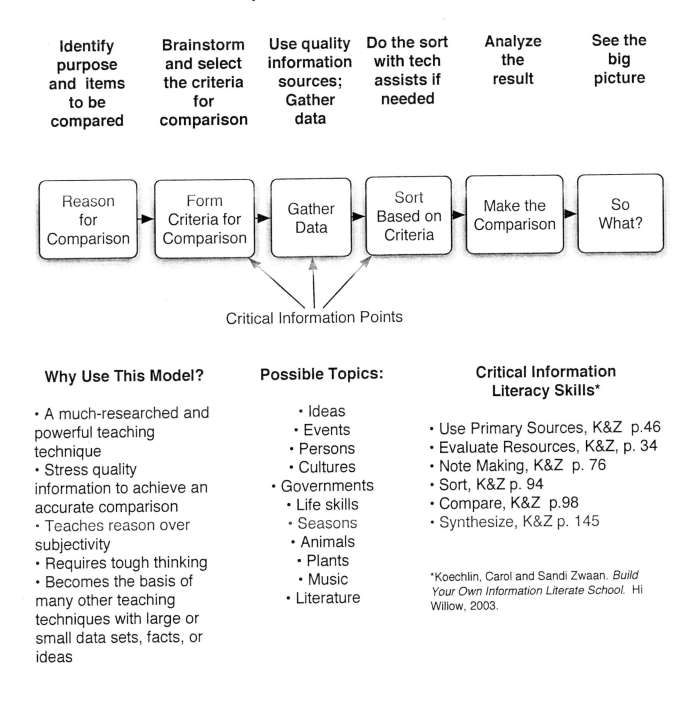

Identify purpose and items to be compared	Brainstorm and select the criteria for comparison	Use quality information sources; Gather data	Do the sort with tech assists if needed	Analyze the result	See the big picture
Reason for Comparison	Form Criteria for Comparison	Gather Data	Sort Based on Criteria	Make the Comparison	So What?

Critical Information Points

Why Use This Model?

• A much-researched and powerful teaching technique
• Stress quality information to achieve an accurate comparison
• Teaches reason over subjectivity
• Requires tough thinking
• Becomes the basis of many other teaching techniques with large or small data sets, facts, or ideas

Possible Topics:

• Ideas
• Events
• Persons
• Cultures
• Governments
• Life skills
• Seasons
• Animals
• Plants
• Music
• Literature

Critical Information Literacy Skills*

• Use Primary Sources, K&Z p.46
• Evaluate Resources, K&Z, p. 34
• Note Making, K&Z p. 76
• Sort, K&Z p. 94
• Compare, K&Z p.98
• Synthesize, K&Z p. 145

*Koechlin, Carol and Sandi Zwaan. *Build Your Own Information Literate School.* Hi Willow, 2003.

Notes on the Compare and Contrast Model

The research backing the use of compare/contrast as an effective teaching strategy is well documented.[1] We may ask students to compare prices at the book store, understand cultural perspectives, or contrast the political events across time periods. In this model, students are asked to choose a reason for comparison, gather data, and then form criteria for comparison. Such a formulation is often neglected in the compare/contrast models often used.

Although requirements for this skill appear often in learning expectations, it is rarely taught as a skill. A pre-requisite skill for making comparisons is a simple sorting by attribute. Making comparisons is actually a very complex process. Students need to decide what they are comparing and why. They next need to consider which aspects of these items they will examine for purpose of comparison. To decide on criteria for comparison students need to think about which parts are important or will help them with their information problem. Which relationships are important? (E.g. If a student is researching the special survival skills of arctic animals, they may decide to compare the polar bear, the musk ox and the fox. To determine their special survival skills they will need to gather data about specifics such as the animal's coat, sight, habitat, enemies, eating habits and group dynamics. Once they have gathered and categorized data by criteria students will next look for similarities and differences.)

Students are then asked to make a quality comparison by sorting their information according to the criteria. Librarians may want to teach the use of a Venn diagram to help students arrange their information into categories of similarities and differences. Another technique is the use of a T-chart so that students can record the similarities and differences they discover. Handling two or three different information sources will be easy in comparison to coping with a plethora of authorities on a particular topic or issue. In the latter case, students will find it difficult to manage all of the various items to be compared, and will need extra help in organizing their discoveries. For example, they might compare the messages of 25-50 advertisements for any week on television. Their compare/contrast activity will be to notice various propaganda techniques used across types of products. Set down in these terms, what seems to be a difficult challenge results in a narrow subset of possibilities. Even though the number of advertisements might increase to 100 or more, the number of propaganda techniques does not increase measurably as the number of voices increase.

---

[1] See chapter 2: "Identiying Similarities and Differences" in Marzano, Robert J., et. al. A Handbook for Classrom Instruction That Works. ASCD, 2004.

Technology

Sometimes the best technology is the simplest technology such as paper and pencil, Venn diagrams written on the board, or using Post-It notes to help arrange ideas.

For numeric data, spreadsheets, charts, or graphing software might help us compare such things as prices so that the resulting message from the picture offers telling evidence about which car is the best deal, etc.

Research

Marzano[2] makes the following points in summarizing the research on compare and contrast:
1. Presenting students with explicit guidance in identifying similarities and differences enhances students' understanding of and ability to use knowledge.
2. Asking students to independently identify similarities and differences enhances students' understanding of an ability to use knowledge.
3. Representing similarities and differences in graphic or symbolic form enhances students' understanding of and ability to use knowledge.

---

[2] Marzano. *op. cit., p. 15-16.*

Critical Information Skills for Compare and Contrast Model

Use Primary Sources
Students will collect and analyze primary sources of information.

When students are required to conduct an interview or a survey, they are gathering original primary data. When students analyze photographs or artifacts from a time period they are also working with first hand information. Historical primary sources can make the past come alive for students. To optimize these resources students need to learn how to interpret and analyze them. Technology has made it possible to bring many primary artifacts into the classroom virtually.

Evaluate Resources
Students will evaluate resources for usefulness.

Determining whether or not resources are useful and reliable sources of information is a critical step when dealing with volumes of data. Students must first develop an awareness of their information need and then scan the text for evidence of relevance. They must also learn how to validate a resource by checking the contents against determined criteria. They need to realize that not everything they read, hear, and view, is reliable. Students need strategies for examining information sources critically and then lots and lots of practice.

Note Making
Students will develop note making skills and a variety of strategies for organizing the selected data.

Once students have identified and gathered the best sources of information for their inquiry they must prepare to collect the data they need to answer their inquiry question. Students now need to be taught how to identify the information they need and develop a variety of strategies for keeping all this information organized. When students are taking notes from their sources they are already starting to analyze their data.

Sort
Students will sort gathered data for specific purposes.

Sorting is an important entry-level analysis skill. Provide students with tactile/concrete sorting experiences before tackling the sorting of data. E.g. sort pictures, books, stamps, etc. Before students begin to sort, clear purpose and criteria must be established.

Compare
Students will make comparisons to discover relationships in gathered data.

Making comparisons is actually a complex process. Students must first of all determine exactly what is being compared and why, then decide which aspects of the items they will examine for the purposes of comparison. Consequently they need at least two bodies of information and pre-determined criteria to help sort the points of comparison. Once sorted, they need to determine what is similar and what is different.

Synthesize
Students will synthesize information to answer their inquiry question and/or create something new.

Only after careful analysis, can students begin productive synthesis. When they synthesize students take all the parts identified and put them back together again in a new meaningful way. Through synthesis students build understanding and create new personal knowledge.

Examples of the Compare and Contrast Model

Unit 17: Big and Bigger   Gr. 2–4

How are Dinosaurs similar to and different from large animals that live on earth today?
Reason
Students are studying dinosaurs. To help them gain some perspective, have students compare dinosaurs to large animals still found today.
Form Criteria for comparison
Model how to make comparisons using criteria. Provide lots of pictures of dinosaurs as well as large land, sea and air animals of today. Ask students to sort the pictures and then explain which criteria they used for sorting. Chart criteria useful for comparison as students provide it (e.g. short tails, no fur, four legs, live in the water etc.). Together decide on the criteria that will be used for comparing a dinosaur of their choice with a large animal living on earth today (e.g. habitat, food, size, appearance, special survival skills, natural enemies etc.).
Gather Data
Each student decides on the dinosaur and living animal they want to compare. Provide students with the organizer *Digging for Facts.* Ensure that students have access to material at their reading level and/or arrange for learning buddies to assist them. Students gather the needed facts based on the criteria for comparison.
Sort Based on Criteria
Have students circle and join similarities with a colored marker or highlighter. All the other facts are different.
So What?
Have students make a pattern booklet
................is similar to a ....because ....
................is different than a ....because ....

Unit 18: Natural Designers   Gr. 4–8

How has nature provided models for engineering and design?
Reason for Comparison
Science and Technology classes are beginning a study of design. Look first at the purpose and function of design in nature and then have students find a manmade application of that design and work out a metaphor. Review metaphors and examine lots of samples.
Form Criteria
Introduce by showing pictures of such things as a swallow's nest, magnified insect wing, an ant colony etc. Have students brainstorm for other fascinating designs in nature. Select an example of a metaphor in nature and model development for students. e.g. a honeycomb and a large apartment complex. Chart things that are the same and things that are different. Examine the chart and cluster items to develop criteria that could be used for making comparisons between natural and man made structures (e. g. design, material, purpose, structure, and origin).
Gather Data
Students conduct searches to find designs in nature. Have students develop a list of key words and search terms they could use to access the data they need. Once students have a collection of natural designs they need to work on matching them with a man made design e.g. burdock burrs and Velcro.
Sort
Form small groups. Ask students to select an example from the generated list of natural and man made designs that they want to compare. Using the organizer *What's the Same? What's Different?* . Have students apply criteria for comparison and complete their analysis.
So What?
Students can use the organizer to assist with development of a poem or visual that elaborates on the metaphor.

Unit 19: Grading Schools   Gr. 10–12

Which post-secondary educational facilities are best for me?

Reason
This activity will help students to research and analyze data to enable them to find the schools that are best for them after finishing secondary education.

Form Criteria
In groups have students brainstorm for the things they will look for in a post secondary school. Share and chart their ideas. Cluster similar ideas and develop a set of criteria for assessing the suitability of prospective schools. E.g. academic programs, fees, scholarships, admission requirements, web service, access to library, distance education, athletics, recreation, housing, virtual tour, disability services, bookstore, location, transportation links etc. Individual students will consider items in the criteria list and make note of their personal requirements with regard to each criterion. E.g. must be on a bus route that links with home, must offer secondhand texts for sale, would like an Olympic sized pool on campus or nearby.

Gather Data
Provide students with the URLs of state/province wide post secondary institutions or instruct students to conduct their own searches if time permits. Have them search these sites to discover data to satisfy each criterion and then enter the data in a searchable database.

Sort based on criteria
Using the database software students can sort and compare the collected data. Students experiment with several kinds of graphs and charts to select those that best illustrate their analysis.

So What?
Each student selects a few schools of interests and puts together a portfolio of graphs and data to present to his/her family. Students may use an organizer such as the *School Selection: So What?* worksheet to help when discussing their future plans with their parents.

Gathering Evidence of Understanding
- appropriate criteria set
- adequate, relevant data gathered
- data successfully entered in database
- a good variety of graphs and charts that show effective comparisons
- schools selected are appropriate for student

InfoSkills
- use primary sources - gather from virtual resources
- sort
- compare - student criteria and organizing tool
- synthesis - make a decision

Reflect, Rethink, Redesign
- Did students have access to sufficient resources to meet their needs? If not how could I facilitate broader access?
- Were students' criteria realistic and practical? What could be done to help them with realism in this regard?
- How have I/could I further involve the guidance staff?
- Would a set of prompts for pre activity with discussions with parents be helpful?
- What is the student level of skill with databases? Should I arrange database tutorials for some students?
- Are special arrangements required so students can save and print their graphs and charts?
- What can I do to accommodate/assist students who are not considering post secondary education?

Digging for Facts

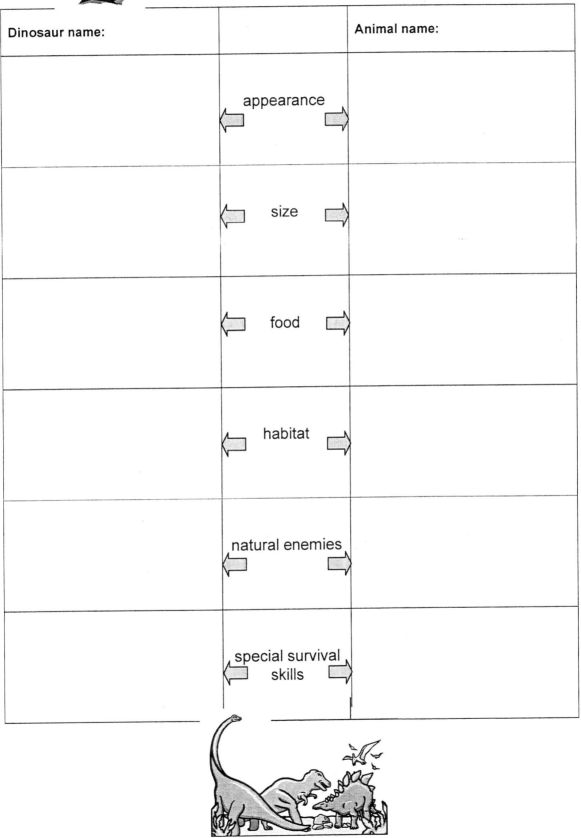

Dinosaur name:		Animal name:
	appearance	
	size	
	food	
	habitat	
	natural enemies	
	special survival skills	

What's the Same? What's Different?

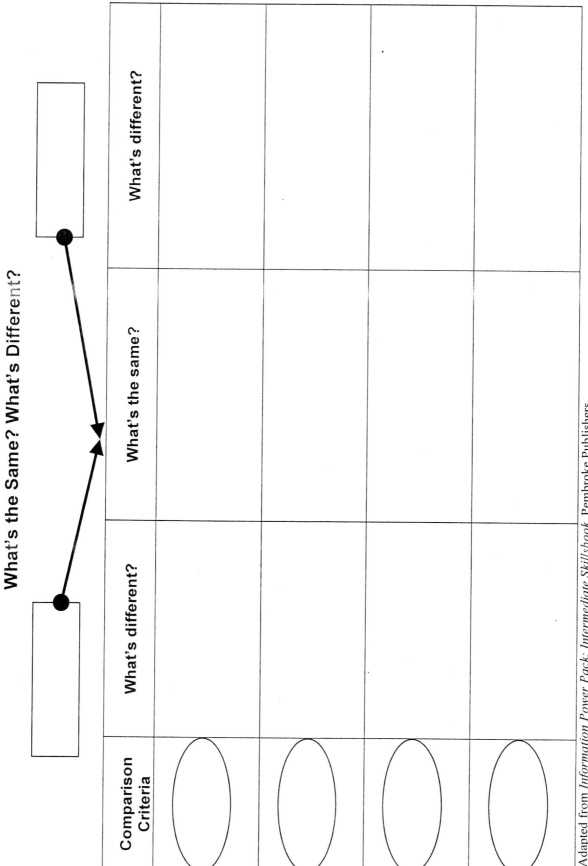

Comparison Criteria	What's different?	What's the same?	What's different?

Adapted from *Information Power Pack: Intermediate Skillsbook*, Pembroke Publishers

74   Compare and Contrast Model

School Selection: So What?

Take a closer look at the shools you selected. Consider them using these prompts.

Selection Criteria

Schools	Must Haves	Would Like to Have
School # 1		
School # 2		
School # 3		

Schools	Pros	Cons
School # 1		
School # 2		
School # 3		

Do these schools really meet the selection criteria you and your parents have?
Should you go back and reconsider some others?

Part Two

The Main Course:

Concept Jigsaw Puzzle Model

The Concept Jigsaw Puzzle Model

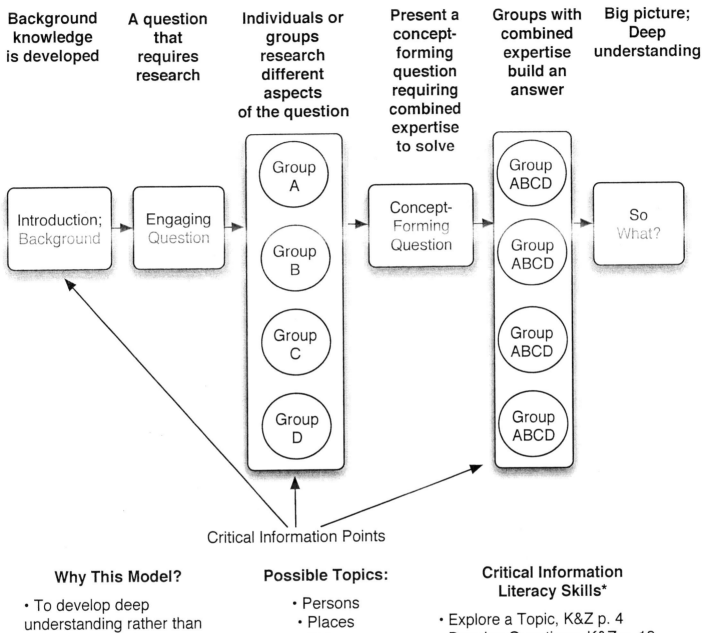

Background knowledge is developed — **A question that requires research** — **Individuals or groups research different aspects of the question** — **Present a concept-forming question requiring combined expertise to solve** — **Groups with combined expertise build an answer** — **Big picture; Deep understanding**

Introduction; Background → Engaging Question → [Group A, Group B, Group C, Group D] → Concept-Forming Question → [Group ABCD, Group ABCD, Group ABCD, Group ABCD] → So What?

Critical Information Points

Why This Model?

- To develop deep understanding rather than surface knowledge
- To develop group skills
- Two heads are better than one
- A prototype of the real world of business and industry
- To stimulate each learner into making a contribution
- Use to introduce lots of material quickly

Possible Topics:

- Persons
- Places
- Things
- Events
- Ideas
- Movements

Critical Information Literacy Skills*

- Explore a Topic, K&Z p. 4
- Develop Questions, K&Z p. 12
- Locate Resources, K&Z p. 28
- Evaluate Resources, K&Z p. 34
- Collaborate, K&Z p. 140

* Koechlin, Carol and Sandi Zwaan. *Build Your Own Information Literate School.* Hi Willow, 2003

Notes on the Concept Jigsaw Puzzle Model

The jigsaw puzzle model asks students to become an expert about a topic and then combine their expertise with others to form a big picture or gain deeper understanding. For a good jigsaw, select one or several state standards that require detailed topical knowledge and critical thinking. Look for standards that require skills in using, finding, sorting, and analyzing information. Then build an assessment that combines both the content and the process knowledge.

At the beginning of the concept jigsaw, if students have very little background knowledge, use library resources to build that background—particularly for students with language problems or differing cultural experiences. Simple books with lots of pictures, encyclopedias, and multimedia materials might help. Develop a question that will lead students to collect information about a subtopic such as a state, a person, an event, an animal, or a particular literary work. The more the student learns about the subtopic the better. Choice in information resources is critical at this point since students will have differing abilities, learning styles, and interest levels. Actual documents, notes, and paraphrases can all be organized at this point to answer the first question posed. There could also be a finished product at stage one such as a worksheet, report, or multimedia product complete with correct citations and a bibliography of information resources used.

Stopping at the first stage is a common practice in education. Students turn in their reports or give them orally in class; they demonstrate their knowledge of the subtopic they studied (a tiger or the state of Iowa), but know little about the larger topic of animals or other American states. Another problem is the amount of cutting, clipping, and plagiarism that has become legendary in the age of the Internet. Students given a choice of topic with the assignment "do a report or term paper" are tempted to cut and clip something from the Internet or library resources and turn it in as their own work. The concept jigsaw negates the temptation to cut and clip. It challenges students to combine their expertise with other student mini-experts to develop a larger view or deeper understanding. No matter where the information has come from, students suddenly realize that they must *understand* the information in order to be a participant in phase two—the actual jigsaw.

For the jigsaw activity, the development of a second higher-level question is critical. New groups of students, each with a different expertise, are directed to confront a tough and challenging question. A compare/contrast activity requires students to learn what others know and then combine that knowledge with their own. This will require both the teacher and the librarian to teach skills of compare/contrast, summation, analysis, and synthesis. The jigsaw works because "I as a learner combine my piece of the puzzle with other pieces to make sense of a larger issue or concept."

In summary, students have used an information-rich environment to build background knowledge and to become a mini-expert in a subtopic. They then use that information to think about, compare, and develop a wider, more synthesized understanding of their topic. The concept jigsaw will work well if students seriously pursue their individual subtopics, assemble high quality information, and bring an understanding of that information to the second round of the jigsaw. A narrow range of information or poor quality information will cause errors of judgment and an erroneous or faulty conclusion at the end.

Technology

Numerous technology tools are useful in the concept jigsaw model. Utilizing the online library catalog, library databases, and full Internet searches using search engines will provide a plethora of information on the students' subtopics at a level they can read and understand. Other technology tools can be used to take notes, copy extracts, concept map, and correctly cite the sources students are using.

Collaborative technologies such as teleconferencing, videoconferencing, web boards, and online discussions can assist students working in groups whether in the same school or located anywhere in the world. Developing rapidly are software programs that allow group creation of a product such as Group-Office, Blackboard, and WebCT.

Presentation software such as PowerPoint, KeyNote, and Apple's iLife suite will stimulate creativity and intense interest if the emphasis is on the message rather than the glitz of presentation.

Research

For a review of the research on cooperative learning, an essential component of the jigsaw, see chapter seven of Marzano's[1] book: "Cooperative Learning" pages 84-91.

---

[1] Marzano, Robert J., Debra J. Pickering, and Jane E. Pollock. *Classroom Instruction that Works: Research-Based Strategies for Increasing Student Achievement.* ASCD, 2004.

Critical Information Skills for
Concepts Jigsaw Puzzle Model

Explore a Topic
Students will use a variety of strategies to explore a topic in preparation for research.

This first step in research is crucial to research success. Students are often discouraged by research projects because they find the topic too broad, too narrow or of no personal interest. Engage students and fire up their passion and curiosity. Provide them with a good working knowledge of the topic so they can create questions or select effective keywords and become familiar with the language of the topic. The time spent up front with exploration activities will pay huge dividends later in the research cycle.

Develop Questions
Students will develop effective questions to guide their research.

Research is the question. Successful research projects are dependant on the quality of the question(s). To be able to think critically about a topic, students need to develop effective questions to guide the research process. They need questions that drive analysis. The secret to developing good research questions is providing the students with rich exploratory experiences so they can wonder about the topic. If students are thus stimulated, natural curiosity should take over and a flurry of questions will be generated. Helping students become more conscious of the kinds of questions they formulate and helping them realize which questions will generate high-level critical thinking is the next challenge.

Locate Resources
Students will locate resources relevant to their defined need.

Students must know where different types of material are located and how to access the specific resources they need for their inquiries and interests. Students who are proficient at locating resources are able to devote more time to selecting and processing the data they find. We must design meaningful activities in the context of current curriculum to facilitate development of locating skills.

Evaluate Resources
Students will evaluate resources for usefulness.

Info-glut is a major problem for young researches. Students must first develop an awareness of their information need and then scan the text for evidence of relevance. They must also learn how to validate a resource by checking the contents against determined criteria. Students need strategies for examining information resources critically as well as lots and lots of practice in applying them. Eventually, evaluation of recreational reading material and information resources will become a natural step in their selection process.

Collaborate
Students will collaborate to enhance their understanding of information.

Collaborative learning is an instructional strategy in which students work in groups toward a common academic goal. Group work creates a powerful synergy in your classroom. Purposeful talk can enrich the processes of brainstorming, questioning, analysis, problem solving, evaluating, creating and communicating information. While working effectively in groups is a valuable skill in the world of academics, it is also high on the list of employability skills and much sought after in the world of business.

Examples of the Concept Jigsaw Model
Unit 20: Just Like Me   Gr. 1–3

Background: Over a number of days, read aloud carefully selected stories about children of other countries. Show and discuss pictures and videos of children living in other countries. Discuss with your students how these children are the same as they are.

JigSaw: *How are we all the same?*			
Specialist Team		**Sharing Team**	
First Question: *What is life like for children in another country?*	**Research:** Organize small groups of four. Each of these Specialist Teams will research the life of children in another country. Provide students with *My Research Organizer* on which to record their discoveries. Modify for students with low language acquisition by pairing them up with an adult volunteer or learning buddy and/or having them illustrate their information.	**Concept Forming Question:** *What do the children from these countries have in common?*	**JigSaw:** One student from each Specialist Team joins the new Sharing Team. Students share their expert information about the country they studied in their Specialist Team. Students discuss the life of children from each of the four countries and identify any common elements. They record each common element on a card.
Group A - Country A		Group ABCD	
Group B - Country B		Group ABCD	
Group C - Country C		Group ABCD	
Group D - Country D		Group ABCD	

So What? Post the cards developed by the sharing teams, discuss and cluster the common elements. Develop a list of things that are common to children all around the world. Provide opportunities for students to apply this new concept creatively (e.g. mural, drama, clay model, painting, or story).

Unit 21: Women in the Media   Gr. 10–12

Background: Explore the imaging of women over the ages in North America using archival photos, music, art and video.

JigSaw: Does media affect the imaging of women?			
Specialist Team		**Sharing Team**	
First Question: *How are women portrayed through the media in North American society today?*	**Research:** Organize groups of four. Each Specialist Team researches the imaging of women through a popular cultural medium. Provide students with *Keeping Organized* worksheet for recording their discoveries.	**Concept Forming Question:** *Are there any common patterns or trends in the imaging of women in popular culture today?*	**JigSaw:** One student from each Specialist Team joins the new Sharing Team. Students share their expert information about the cultural medium they researched. Students discuss their findings, look for patterns or trends, and identify any common elements. They record each common element on a card.
Group A - movies		Group ABCD	
Group B - music		Group ABCD	
Group C - sports		Group ABCD	
Group D - advertising		Group ABCD	

So What? Post the cards developed by the Sharing Teams; discuss and cluster the common elements. Develop a list of common images of women today. Have students return to their Specialist Team and discuss their impressions of whether or not the imaging of women has changed over time. Why or why not? Jigsaw again in their Sharing Team and discuss the impact media has had on the imaging of women over time. Students develop questions for further independent study or prepare a creative expression of their findings.

Unit 22: Global Citizens   Gr. 8–10

Global Citizens *Who is responsible for care of our planet? What are the responsibilities of individuals and countries with regard to global issues? What is understood by the term "global citizen"?*

Background: Introduce the concept of global issue by reading and discussing *If the World Were a Village* by David Smith. Brainstorm to identify organized groups with global concerns. Select specific groups for this study.

First Question: *What are the roles and responsibilities of global organizations?*

JigSaw:

Specialist Team	
Group A - United Nations	Group D - International Red Cross
Group B - World Wildlife Association	Group E - World Health Organization
Group C - World Watch	

Research: Organize groups of five. Each Specialist Team researches a global organization in terms of their roles and responsibilities and history. Have students create a triple T-Chart organizer for recoding their discoveries.

Concept Forming Question: *What are the responsibilities of individuals and countries with regard to global issues? What is understood by the term "global citizen"?*

JigSaw:

Sharing Team	
Group ABCDE	Group ABCDE
Group ABCDE	Group ABCDE
Group ABCDE	

One student from each Specialist Team joins the new Sharing Team. Students present their expert information about the global organization they researched. Using the *Global Organization* worksheet group records key points. Ask groups to identify the scope of concerns and discuss and formulate some ideas about responsibilities. With this background, discuss the roles and responsibilities of individuals and countries, with regard to global issues. Work together to develop a definition for the term "global citizen".

So What?

Students could select a topic or issue for further study, develop a creative interpretation of the term *global citizen,* or take some informed action on a global issue they are interested in or concerned about.

Gathering Evidence of Understanding
- Students evaluate and select relevant resources.
- Specialist teams accurately identify and chart roles and responsibilities of their organization.
- Teams share information so others are able to engage in meaningful discussion regarding responsibilities of individuals and countries.
- Students develop a meaningful definition for the term "global citizen".

Info Skills
- explore a topic
- locate resources
- evaluate resources
- use organizers
- collaborate
- make connections

Reflect, Rethink, Redesign

- Did the organizations we chose to research provide a broad look at global issues?
- Were all teams able to find the quality and quantity of information required? If not, how could the teacher, librarian and I help?
- Could the students move back and forth in to their teams with ease? Why or Why not?
- Was group collaboration effective in all teams? Which worked well? Why?
- Could teams with effective collaboration share some ideas to help others?
- How did this strategy help students develop the concept of a "global citizen"?
- Which students are motivated to take some "informed action"? What was the catalyst for these students?

My Research Organizer

We want to find out about children in..................
We used
- ☐ books
- ☐ pictures
- ☐ videos
- ☐ computers

How are we all the same?

Family Life	School
Playing	**Clothing**
Homes	**Special Days**

Pictures

Keeping Organized

How are women portrayed in the media in North American society today?

Source :	
Notes	Quotes

Source :	
Notes	Quotes

Source :	
Notes	Quotes

Source :	
Notes	Quotes

Global Organization

Who is responsible for care of our planet?

Organization:

Roles	Responsibilities

Organization:

Roles	Responsibilities

Organization:

Roles	Responsibilities

Organization:

Roles	Responsibilities

Organization:

Roles	Responsibilities

Organization:

Roles	Responsibilities

The Problems/Possibilities
Jigsaw Puzzle Model

The Problems/Possibilities Jigsaw Puzzle Model

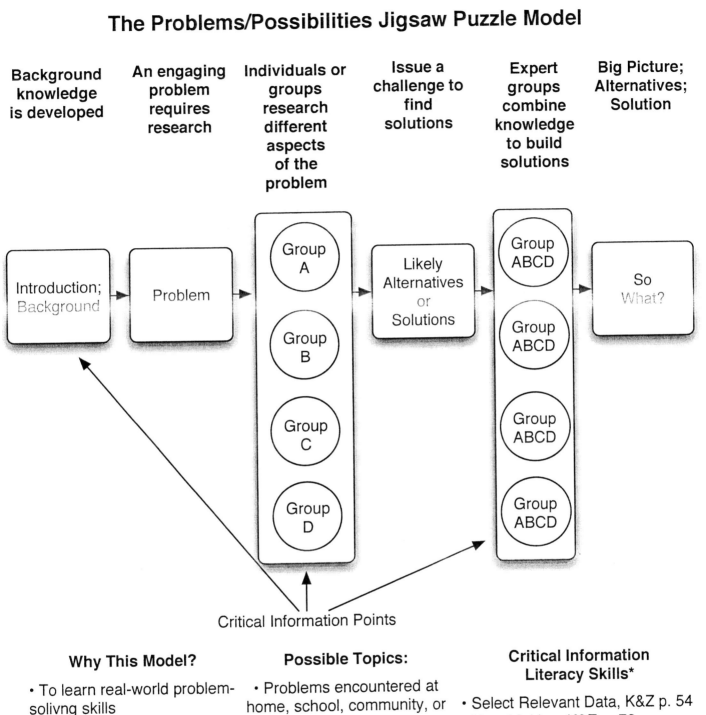

Background knowledge is developed — **An engaging problem requires research** — **Individuals or groups research different aspects of the problem** — **Issue a challenge to find solutions** — **Expert groups combine knowledge to build solutions** — **Big Picture; Alternatives; Solution**

Introduction; Background → Problem → Group A / Group B / Group C / Group D → Likely Alternatives or Solutions → Group ABCD / Group ABCD / Group ABCD / Group ABCD → So What?

Critical Information Points

Why This Model?

- To learn real-world problem-solivng skills
- Build group problem-solving skills
- A prototype of the real world of business and industry
- To stimulate each learner into making a contribution
- To encourage investigation, determination, and perserverence

Possible Topics:

- Problems encountered at home, school, community, or nation
- Society problems such as poverty or health care
- Real problems created from learning experiences or projects

Critical Information Literacy Skills*

- Select Relevant Data, K&Z p. 54
- Note Making, K&Z p. 76
- Collaborate, K&Z p. 140
- Make Connections, K&Z p.116
- Synthesize, K&Z p. 145

* Koechlin, Carol and Sandi Zwaan. *Build Your Own Information Literate School.* Hi Willow, 2003

Notes on the Problems/Possibilities
Jigsaw Puzzle Model

Problem solving is a lifelong skill sought after by many organizations, businesses, and governments. When a complex problem arises, bosses tend to bring in larger numbers of persons with various expertises to either recommend or discover solutions. The classic line in the Hollywood film "Apollo 13" is "Houston, we have a problem." Expertise, time pressure, and creativity join to save a critical mission and the lives of the astronauts. This contrasts with the Challenger mission where the problem was not ascertained until long after the disaster had happened.

Teaching students the problem-solving skills they will need to succeed in school and beyond will work best when students are presented with real or relevant problems. If the issue is engaging and perhaps personal to them or their interests, they will be more enthusiastic about working toward a solution.

Once a problem has been selected, it is wise to spend time in the library building background so that the students can begin studying the problem with efficiency and earnest. Background will include knowledge of the subject at hand, as well as instruction in the act of problem solving. For the latter, students might watch the "Apollo 13" movie segment and then brainstorm the steps the experts used to conquer something that seemed impossible at the time. For the problem at hand, students should determine what expertise they will need to develop possible ways to attack the problem and find possible sources of information/expertise they might call upon in their own quest. The librarian will be a key source of help to seek, sort, and sift through critical information.

As students are regrouped and confront the second and more difficult problem, they will need to mine the expertise of each member of their new group; learn to analyze what they know and what they need to know; and apply creativity and synthesis as they progress. Over time, the spirit of competition among the new groups will increase motivation and push the work ethic. For example, many high school and college students face the group challenge of creating a robot that will survive some sort of battle or conflict. Such episodes are memorable for all participants.

There are many fascinating topics: Who can write the solution to a mystery story that solves the crime using the most authentic science? (You may discover some budding Pat Cornwells.) Which student's plan for the reconstruction of the school's playground provides the best result for the least amount of money? What plan for school safety will balance our sense of freedom vs. feeling like we are in prison all day? The most compelling problems will require students to collect and analyze quality information from the best and most trusted sources. They will also need to combine this information with their own best thinking and creativity. The challenge, of course, is to keep exciting problems and questions within a reasonable time frame since they tend to expand as excitement and challenge build.

Technology

Technology tools are extremely useful in the investigation and resolution of problems. One might use an office package containing word processors, spreadsheets and presentation tools, or other computer software that creates organizational charts, flow charts, or Gantt charts to help organize and manage different facets of the problem. Telecommunications systems such as teleconferencing, e-mail, or group discussion boards will be invaluable in tapping into expertise beyond the school. Don't overlook online databases and the full Internet (including blogs) as authoritative sources.

Research

For a review of the research on cooperative learning, an essential component of the jigsaw, see chapter seven of Marzano's[1] book: "Cooperative Learning" pages 84-91.

---

[1] Marzano, Robert J., Debra J. Pickering, and Jane E. Pollock. *Classroom Instruction that Works: Research-Based Strategies for Increasing Student Achievement.* ASCD, 2004.

Critical Information Skills for Problems/Possibilities Jigsaw Model

---

Select Relevant Data

Students will identify and select relevant data from a variety of non-fiction resources and record the key points.

At this stage of the process students are examining sources and applying their active reading, viewing and listening skills to hunt for those nuggets of information that will help them with their quest. They need to explore the ideas of others before they can start to build their own understanding. Extracting the relevant data, recording it accurately and keeping it in a safe place until they are ready to process it is the aim of this exercise. Relevance, accuracy, precision and academic honesty are key elements.

Note Making

Students will develop note making skills and a variety of strategies for organizing the selected data.

Once students have identified and gathered the best sources of information for their inquiry they must prepare to collect the data they need to answer their inquiry question. Students now need to be taught how to identify the information they need and develop a variety of strategies for keeping all this information organized. When students are taking notes from their sources they are already starting to analyze their data.

Collaborate

Students will collaborate to enhance their understanding of information.

Collaborative learning is an instructional strategy in which students work in groups toward a common academic goal. Group work creates a powerful synergy in your classroom. Purposeful talk can enrich the processes of brainstorming, questioning, problem solving, evaluating, creating and communicating information. While working effectively in groups is a valuable skill in the world of academics it also high on the list of employability skills and much sought after in the world of business.

Make Connections

Students will work with information to make connections.

There are many "connection building" strategies we can teach to help students understand content. When we suggest that students make connections we want them to make links to what they already know. What they know about the topic, what they know about reading (viewing/listening) strategies, what they know about webbing/mapping, and how this new content fits into their personal experiences.

Synthesize

Students will synthesize information to answer their inquiry question and/or create something new.

Only after careful analysis can students begin productive synthesis. When they synthesize students take all the parts identified and put them back together again in a new meaningful way. Through synthesis students build understanding and create new personal knowledge.

Examples of the Problem/Possibilities Jigsaw Puzzle Model

Unit 23: Investigate the Swamp behind the School   Gr. 6–8

The swamp stinks; the neighbors complain; the city is about to pave it over. Stop. The sixth grade classes volunteer to study the problem under the direction of their teachers and librarian. The problem is first attacked by teams of specialists, then they jigsaw to form competitive teams to develop and propose a solution.

6th Graders Attack the Swamp Problem			
Specialist Teams	New Groups Formed	Competitive Team Solutions	Presentations to Community and Government for Resolution
Team A: History of swamp		Team 1: (ABCD)	
Team B: Government/community relations		Team 2: (ABCD)	
Team C: Ecology of swamp		Team 3: (ABCD)	
Team D: Alternatives across the country		Team 4: (ABCD)	
Etc.		Etc.	

Each specialist team must do thorough research to build expertise before competitive teams are formed. Presentations will be to real community groups and councils.[1] Final presentations must be realistic, contain budget projections, and propose timelines.

Unit 24: Investigate Diseases of Our Peers   Gr. 9–12

With news of fellow students' major health problems, a class wonders what can be done. Specialist teams under the direction of the teacher and librarian research each disease of interest. Quality and expert information during the research is stressed.

Freshmen Attack Diseases of Their Peers			
Specialist Teams	New Groups Formed	Team Solutions	School Campaign for Understanding and Career Fair for Medicine and Health
Team A: Meningitis		Team 1: (ABCD)	
Team B: West Nile Virus		Team 2: (ABCD)	
Team C: HIV/AIDS		Team 3: (ABCD)	
Team D: Manic Depression/Suicide		Team 4: (ABCD)	
Etc.		Etc.	

With expertise in a single disease, new teams combine their knowledge looking for patterns, possibilities for informing fellow students, and some way to help.[2]

---

[1] One such real problem done in a middle school in Aurora, Colorado discovered that the swamp was part of an original bird flyway over the city. The solution was to restore the swamp to attract birds. It happened.

[2] At Newsome Park Elementary School in Newport News, Virginia, second graders curious about the number of medicines a classmate takes and her frequent trips to the doctor investigated (with the classmate's permission) the causes of cystic fibrosis. They invited experts to tell them about the disease, wrote up their research, used graphs and PowerPoint® to tell the story, sold pledges to and participated in a cystic fibrosis walkathon.

Make Your Own Ending   Gr. 2–4

What is the best ending for this story?

Background
Select a picture book that has an overt problem in the story. E.g. Humphrey the Lost Whale by Wendy Tokuda and Richard Hall. Examine the cover of book and ask students to predict what the storybook is about.

Problem
Explain to students that this book is based on a real story. Read the story to the point where the big problem is revealed. Humphrey is upstream caught behind the Golden Gate Bridge in San Francisco Bay and he can't get back under the bridge. What can be done to save Humphrey?

Research
Organize the students in groups. They will work at centers organized by resource type. Students use *Mission Notes* to guide their research on humpbacks whales, their survival needs, other incidents of stranded humpbacks and rescue missions. When the research group data has been gathered, create the problem solving groups with one expert from each research group. This new group will brainstorm for possible solutions and use *Problems, Problems* worksheet to guide them as they decide what they think is the best way to rescue Humphrey.

Research Group	Problem Solving Group
Group A Non-fiction books	Group ABCD
Group B Encyclopedias	Group ABCD
Group C selected Internet sites	Group ABCD
Group D children's magazines or video	Group ABCD

So What?
Ask each group to present and defend their best solution based on the facts they were able to gather. Finish reading the book and compare student solutions to the one that worked. Evaluate collaboration using Hurrah for Our Team. This story is one of the Reading Rainbow video series. The video extensions will spark further investigations about the fascinating Humpback whale and other whale species.

Gathering Evidence of Understanding
- data selected was accurate, adequate, on topic
- students worked effectively in their groups
- students self assess using *Hurrah for Our Team*
- brainstormed lots of ideas for saving Humphrey
- ideas were weighed against information collected
- best solutions were logical

Info Skills
- select relevant data
- note-making
- collaborate
- make connections
- synthesize - solve a problem

Reflect, Rethink, Redesign
- Are students comfortable and confident working in groups? Should I review guidelines for group work before they begin?
- Did all groups make good notes? How did the organizer help them focus on needed information?
- Are there students who require more structure? How can I help them?
- Did students look at their data for clues when brainstorming possible rescue strategies?
- What strategies did students use to make connections between the data they collected and potential rescue solutions? Which were most successful? Could other students benefit from hearing how these students approached the task? How can I facilitate that sharing?
- What role did questioning play in the process? Did students ask good questions? Are there students who need some help with questioning skills
- Were groups able to explain and support their solutions with data and logic?

Mission Notes "Saving Humphrey"

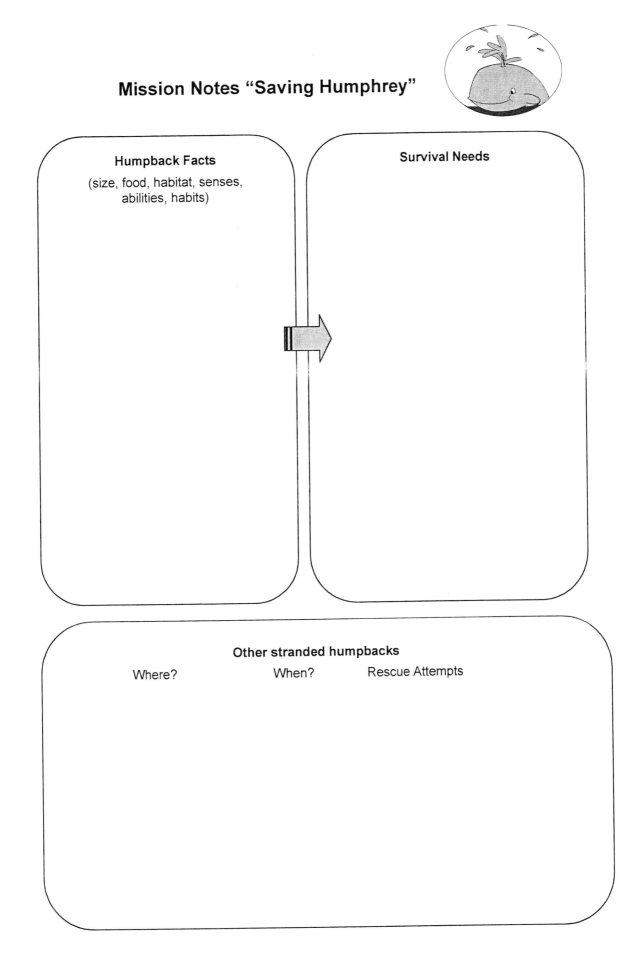

Humpback Facts

(size, food, habitat, senses, abilities, habits)

Survival Needs

Other stranded humpbacks

Where?   When?   Rescue Attempts

Problems, Problems

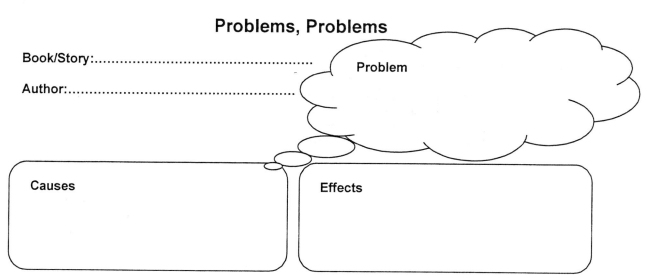

Book/Story:...

Author:...

Problem

Causes

Effects

Solution Ideas	Strengths	Weaknesses
1)		
2)		
3)		
4)		
5)		
6)		
The best solution idea....		

Hurrah for Our Team

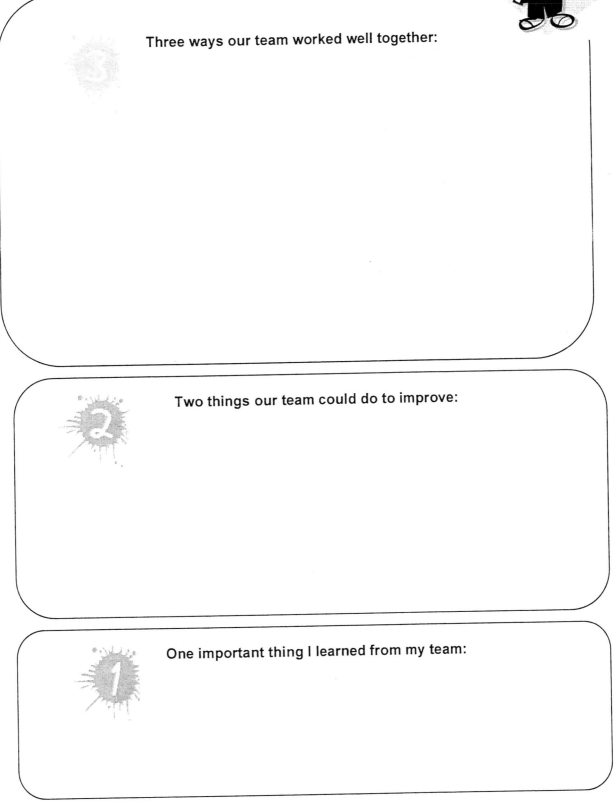

Three ways our team worked well together:

Two things our team could do to improve:

One important thing I learned from my team:

The Matrix Model

The Matrix Model

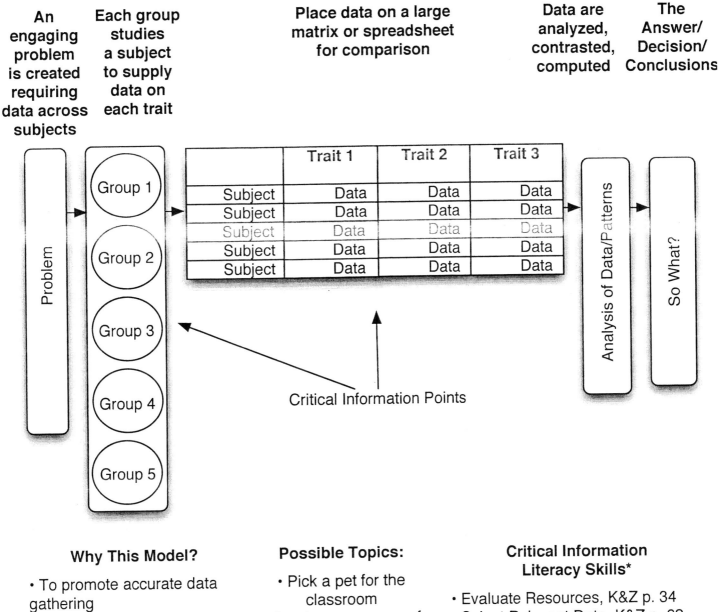

An engaging problem is created requiring data across subjects

Each group studies a subject to supply data on each trait

Place data on a large matrix or spreadsheet for comparison

Data are analyzed, contrasted, computed

The Answer/ Decision/ Conclusions

Problem

Group 1

Group 2

Group 3

Group 4

Group 5

	Trait 1	Trait 2	Trait 3
Subject	Data	Data	Data
Subject	Data	Data	Data
Subject	Data	Data	Data
Subject	Data	Data	Data
Subject	Data	Data	Data

Analysis of Data/Patterns

So What?

Critical Information Points

Why This Model?

- To promote accurate data gathering
- Organizing data for better decisionmaking or understanding
- Facilitating a look at patterns and trends
- Seeing the dangers of bad data in any cell
- Teaching complex issues; solving complex problems

Possible Topics:

- Pick a pet for the classroom
- Are there weapons of mass destruction?
- Comparison of possible new highways
- Comparison of expert opinions about a topic
- Comparison of candidates for office
- Comparing topics of interest

Critical Information Literacy Skills*

- Evaluate Resources, K&Z p. 34
- Select Relevant Data, K&Z p. 62
- Legal and Ethical Use of Information and Ideas, K&Z p. 82
- Share and Use, K&Z p. 156
- Reflect, Transfer and Apply, K&Z p. 166

* Koechlin, Carol and Sandi Zwaan. *Build Your Own Information Literate School*. Hi Willow, 2003

Notes on the Matrix Model

The matrix is a powerful learning experience because it helps students make decisions or see patterns and trends based on data rather than on opinions or whims. Life is full of decisions that would benefit from an objective look at quality data: What car should I buy? Are there weapons of mass destruction? What candidate should I vote for? What pet shall we choose for our classroom? How can we as a school be of the most help to those among us with debilitating diseases and disabilities?

The matrix can be useful in any field. We can analyze patterns in literature across various authors or cultures. We can compare the styles of art created in countries at war or cultures where peace reigns. The data gathered from the library or from an actual event will be the first stage in a very high-level and exciting analysis to produce deep understanding. To report raw data without putting it into a matrix—without any analysis or comparison—is to neglect a great learning opportunity and render the data collection time or reporting time almost useless.

In the first stage of the matrix, individuals or small groups research specific traits and characteristics of their assigned topic, making sure the data they collect is accurate. President Bush expected that the CIA, the DEA, Homeland Security, and "Our Man in Baghdad" would give an accurate assessment of whether there were chemical, biological, or nuclear weapons in Iraq. Using that information, If there is a "Yes" in the matrix cell, President Bush will want authoritative data to back that answer. If there is a "No, But Very Soon" answer, then the answering group will need to be able to defend that assessment as well. Should there be bad data in any cell, the decision makers could well make the wrong decision, sending soldiers to war needlessly.

There is nothing more critical to the success of a matrix than to have excellent, high quality data in every cell of the matrix. The librarian will be most anxious to see that students understand how to find, sort, and judge the quality of each entry in the matrix. A typical matrix can have any of the following information:

- Numerical data - to enable calculations for patterns, trends, or answers.
- Facts or short answers - to enable pattern or trend analysis. Elimination of possible decisions is also an important result. (A tiger is illegal, therefore, a tiger cannot be one of our choices.)
- Research papers, position papers, and white papers - to enable expert analysis backed up with substantial evidence so decisions are made rest on sound evidence.

Another major use of the matrix is to help students see the big picture as they begin to see patterns in the various cells. If the topic was 'Picking a classroom pet,' for example, they may see that the larger the animal, the more difficult it is to choose as a classroom pet. Or, if it is really legal to have a tiger cub in the Kindergarten classroom, then everyone is likely to vote for that option. Again, we may ascertain that the various groups making judgments about weapons of mass destruction are telling us what we wanted to hear all along. Making choices is difficult at any stage of life and across all topical areas. We may discover, for example, that many historical and world-changing events were caused by bad data in a critical matrix.

Technology

Technology can often come to the rescue in analyzing data in a matrix. Formulas in a spreadsheet can help us analyze and graph complex data so that answers become obvious. Graphing or charting software can replace complex data with picture representations, which are much easier to analyze. Groupware, allowing several persons to add, revise, or reinterpret data going into a cell, can draw upon the strengths of the group or be the quality control system for data. For example, students might use sophisticated technology of water samples taken from numerous streams to discover that the acid content in the water is responsible for a widespread fish kill.

Access to a wide variety of online databases through school, public, and/or academic libraries will be critical in gathering a great deal of data. Therefore, students will need to understand the principles of searching and retrieving data from a wide variety of databases or search engines if they are to be successful.

Low-level technology will often come to the rescue in actually building the matrix. If the teacher draws the matrix on the board and numbers the cells, students can then use Post-It Notes to write the data they extract from the library sources. They should number each note to correspond with the cell in the matrix. Following a trip to the library, they will stick their notes in the proper cell on the board. At this point, groups of students can analyze a single cell, a row, a column, or a group of cells to summarize, compare/contrast, see patterns/trends, or decide the answer to a question. The first time this technique is used, students might seem confused. However, with a bit of practice, the teacher can guide them to high-level thinking, analysis, and synthesis. If the librarian is included in the analysis of the matrix, clues for teaching students the sound techniques for gathering and sorting information will become apparent.

Critical Information Skills for The Matrix Model

Evaluate Resources
Students will evaluate resources for usefulness.

Determining whether or not resources are useful and reliable sources of information is a critical step when dealing with volumes of data. Students must first develop an awareness of their information need and then scan the text for evidence of relevance. They must also learn how to validate a resource by checking the contents against determined criteria. They need to realize that not everything they read, hear, and view, is reliable. The fact that it is printed or produced in some way doesn't necessarily make it accurate or reliable. Students need strategies for examining information sources critically and lots and lots of practice in applying them.

Select Relevant Data
Students will identify and select relevant data from a variety of non-fiction resources and record the key points.

At this stage of the process, students are examining sources and applying their active reading, viewing and listening skills to hunt for those nuggets of information that will help them with their quest. They need to explore the ideas of others before they can start to build their own understanding. Extracting the relevant data, recording it accurately, and keeping it in a safe place until they are ready to process it is the aim of this exercise. Relevance, accuracy, precision, and academic honesty are key elements.

Legal and Ethical Use of Information and Ideas
Students will understand copyright and use information ethically and legally.

In order to develop a respect for copyright, students must first understand the role fair laws play in supporting creators so that they have the means to continue to create and produce new products. Having done this we can begin to work on developing academic honesty. Develop note-making skills. Teach referencing skills. Provide students with tools and strategies such as source sheets and referencing samples.

Share and Use
Students will share and use their new knowledge and insight.

Ultimately we want students to select the format, create, and present independently. In preparation for this independence, we need teach the process of creating a variety of types of presentation. At first, students will require many experiences where the product/presentation is teacher-selected and teacher-guided. They will build a number of strategies from which to select and to apply as needed. As they accumulate these experiences, we need to clearly define the steps involved and establish criteria for evaluation so that students have a clear understanding of what is expected. Students need guidance and practice so that they can match their content to the best format for delivering their message.

Reflect, Transfer and Apply
Students will reflect on their work, and transfer and apply their learning to new situations.

This stage of the research process marks the end of the immediate information task and sets the stage for further investigations or applications of the new learning. Students must have metacognitive experiences all through the process as well as at the completion of their sharing in order for real learning to occur. Always provide students with clear indicators of success such as rubrics and checklists before research begins.

Examples of the Matrix Model

Unit 26: Choose a Pet for the Classroom   Gr. K–3

The teacher and the librarian want children to have a memorable learning experience choosing a pet, rather than have the experience become a popularity poll. They use the matrix to organize all the information they can find and to help the children make sound, fact-based decisions.

Kindergarteners Choose a Pet for the Classroom Project						
Subject Groups	Traits/Questions to Answer					
	What will it eat?	Will it stink?	What does the zookeeper advise?	What do the 5th graders advise?	Is it legal?	Etc.
Canary						
Gerbil						
Snake						
Tiger						
Etc.						

The teacher and librarian guide the children in their search for pertinent information from the Internet, books, community sources, parents and other children in the school. Once all the information is gathered and placed in the matrix, they learn how to evaluate this information and make informed decisions based upon it. The matrix helps them organize the information for comparison and analysis.[1]

Unit 27: Select a Candidate Based on the Issues   Gr. 10–12

Three candidates are running for President of the United States: a Republican, a Democrat, and an independent. The teacher and librarian agree to have students base their choice on a deep understanding of issues rather than a focus on surface qualities.

Seniors Choose a Candidate for President Based on the Issues						
Subject Groups	Traits/Questions to Answer					
	Economy	Debt	Foreign Policy	Social Security	Education	Etc.
Republican						
Democrat						
Independent						

Student groups do issue papers, interview political leaders, analyze ideas and trends, study campaign advertising, and learn sound decision-making skills.

---

[1] For a video account of an actual Kindergarten class doing this project and then reflecting upon it as fifth graders, watch: Marriott, Cathy. *We Are Information Literate!* Hi Willow Research & Publishing, 2003 (available from http://www.lmcsource.com).

Unit 28: Hurricane Watch   Gr. 7–12

Have major tropical storms become more severe in the last few years?

Problem
View pictures of tropical storm damage from recent hurricanes. Show a video clip such as *Storms* by Discovery. Provide students with small sticky notes and ask them to record a storm word or phrase on each sticky note. Continue brainstorming storm words until time has expired. In small groups of 4–5 have students share their storm ideas. As they talk, have them start to sort ideas into categories on chart paper (e.g. hurricane names, types of storms, descriptive words and phrases etc.). When all the words and phrases are sorted, instruct students to label the categories, creating a web of storm words. Share the storm words and introduce the guiding question.

Data Gathering
Inform groups that they will be assigned to a decade from the period 1900 to the present. Their task is to gather data about the storms during their time period and enter the data in a class database. They need to use accurate, validated data from authoritative sources and keep a well-documented reference list. Discuss how they will measure the severity of a storm and decide on criteria for data collection (e.g. name of storm, date, duration, intensity, category, deaths, property damage, environmental damage). *See note.

Group Dates	Storm Name	Date	Category	Duration	Rainfall	Death Toll	$$$$ Damage
1900–1919							
1920–1939							
1940–1959							
1960–1989							
1990–20??							

Analyze
Instruct groups to manipulate the data in the database and create visual representations of each criterion across the decades on graphs, charts, and plot lines. Review guiding question and make further comparisons.

So What?
Each group prepares a report based on and backed up by data analysis. Presentation could take the form of a magazine article, oral presentation with a slide show, short video, newscast etc. Students could meet in groups to discuss what needs to be done so that people and structures are better prepared to withstand future hurricanes.

Gathering Evidence of Understanding
- o brainstormed words were appropriate and useful
- o data was adequate and accurate
- o source citations were accurate and complete
- o use of database was effective
- o reports were detailed, accurate and effective
- o groups demonstrated good collaborative skills

Info Skills
- o examine and evaluate resources
- o select relevant data
- o legal and ethical use of information - referencing
- o share and use
- o reflect, transfer and apply

Reflect, Rethink, Redesign
- o Did students have sufficient exploratory experience with the topic to brainstorm productively? If not, what other experience could I provide to help them?
- o Do they require copies of referencing worksheets?
- o Would a validating and evaluating worksheet help some of the students identify authoritative sources?
- o Should I arrange for a review of database software use for any of the students?
- o Are there students who have had personal experiences with hurricanes? How could the class benefit from hearing about their experiences? What can I do to facilitate the sharing?
- o Introduce and discuss tools to assess group work skills before groups begin work. Use the *Collaboration Rubric* and *Team Work Debriefing*.

Collaboration Rubric

Achievement Level	Personal Responsibility	Support/ Appreciation	Focus	Problem Solving	Engagement
Level Four	- takes on leadership role - fulfills all aspects of the role - works as part of the team	- facilitates sharing of ideas and information - honors and praises strengths of others - assists others while respecting their roles and responsibilities	- adjusts plan as necessary to facilitate the needs of team - stays on task and reviews topic as necessary - offers positive support to help others to refocus	- is proactive in solving problems - asks probing questions and listens attentively - tests and evaluates solutions - facilitates consensus	- highly motivated - exhibits excitement - plans and works with others
Level Three	- understands personal role - fulfills assigned role duties - contributes fair share to task	- shares ideas and information - open to ideas/ point of view of others - shows awareness/ concern for feelings of others	- focuses on plan and carries it out - focuses on topic throughout task - completes all tasks on time	- uses a variety of strategies to solve problems - considers all solutions - assists others in problem solving	- very interested - positively and actively engaged - organizes task activities
Level Two	- not fully aware of role assigned - carries out some, but not all, role responsibilities - makes a minor contribution	- shares with reluctance - listens to ideas of others on occasion - offers some support to others	- follows plan some of the time - loses focus of topic and/or plan - completes some tasks on time	- unsure how to deal with most problems - usually goes along with suggested solutions - looks to others for help	- exhibits some interest - usually cooperates with others - lacks organizational skills
Level One	- little awareness of team roles - takes no responsibility for role - contribution of little value	- little effort to share information and ideas - works in isolation - offers little support for others	- pays little attention to plan - not focused on topic or task - does not meet timelines	- gives up readily when problems arise - sometimes frustrated by problems - relies on others to solve problems	- shows no interest in activities - has difficulty working with others - is very disorganized

Team Work Debriefing

Everyone on the team had an important job to do.
How well did we do our jobs?

Team spirit

Team effort

Meeting task expectations

Meeting timelines

Quality of our work

Goals for next time

Working as a group helped us to...

The Timeline Model

The Timeline Model

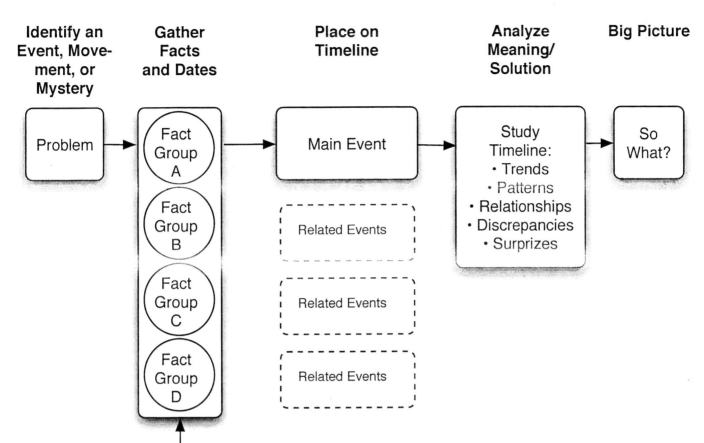

Identify an Event, Movement, or Mystery

Problem

Gather Facts and Dates

Fact Group A

Fact Group B

Fact Group C

Fact Group D

Critical Information Point

Place on Timeline

Main Event

Related Events

Related Events

Related Events

Analyze Meaning/ Solution

Study Timeline:
• Trends
• Patterns
• Relationships
• Discrepancies
• Surprizes

Big Picture

So What?

Why this Model?

• Show changes over time
• Determine why something developed the way it did
• Understand how inaccurate information will distort the analysis of sequencing
• Make comparisons of the past and the present
• Put some events in a larger perspective
• Trace the background to explore cause and effect
• Understand sequence
• Visualize sequential patterns

Possible Topics:

• Chart a political election
• Study a catastrophic event
• Compare various disciplines during a time period
• Reconstruct the events of a crime or event
• Chart the Middle East conflict
• Study the rise of terrorism as warfare
• Chart the plot of a novel or story
• Study the structure of a symphony
• Put a a period of art into its environment
• Study what made landing on the moon possible
• Chart the immigration of a family to the U.S.

Critical Information Literacy Skills*

• Actively Read, View & Listen, K&Z p. 56
• Select Relevant Data, K&Z p. 62
• Sort, K&Z p. 94
• Note Making, K&Z p. 76
• Identify and Investigate Patterns and Trends, K&Z p. 108

*Koechlin, Carol and Sandi Zwaa. *build Your Own Information Literate School*. Hi Willow, 2003

Notes on the Timeline Model

The use of timelines or sequencing as an organizing principle works extremely well in an information-rich environment where the amount of information is too large to keep in the head for sense-making. We often expect the youngest of children to understand time sequencing: we will be going to grandma's house tomorrow, or we were there yesterday and can tell what happened.

Ordering events often helps us understand not only what happened, but also why it happened. For example, strict airport security systems developed because of the events of "9/11." Mapping billions of pieces of weather information in a time sequence helps us understand tornados and hurricanes as they form, move, and dissipate. We expect that children, as they come to school, begin to sequence ideas, particularly in the stories they hear and struggle to read. We often ask students to log steps in a chemistry experiment to help discover why their concoction exploded or turned green instead of red. The more data we are able to chart into a timeline, the more we are able to develop perspective—seeing things in larger contexts with connections to societies, cultures, world events, and civilizations. We ask students to develop a sense of history: why and how our form of democracy emerged and why it is worth preserving.

Genealogy, one of the most popular hobbies in the world, provides people with a sense of identity, and in the modern world of medicine, begins to explain why we are prone to heart attacks or macular degeneration. Extending into the real world, sequence and time affect everything we do from going to work in the morning, constructing a new building, or electing a new president. We demand that students be able to organize events, data, and ideas into timelines to bring order into the world of understanding.

As a teaching technique, timelines help students research, chart, order, and then understand a stream of events and related events. We may chart the progress of technology during the 1980's when the microcomputer was on its fast march toward ubiquity, and we can chart at the same time, the related fields of science, politics, music and art that helped the computer become a common tool for our society.

As students encounter data from many sources to construct their timelines, they will find discrepancies, inaccuracies, and other problems that make the task of building a timeline more complicated, and a challenge ripe for investigation. They will discover plain errors; intentional misrepresentations; honest interpretations of events from different perspectives of people; faulty instrumentation; or new instrumentation that measures events over time more accurately than previous instruments did. In all fields, students will need to discern the accuracy of time measures and how these affect our understanding of the world. For example, it took 300 years to solve the problem of measuring longitude; it was finally solved when a near-perfect clock was invented. Students accustomed to geo-positioning systems often can only appreciate the sailor's fear of longitude when they understand a sequence of events.

Students might be introduced to chronologies—reference books of timelines—in the library reference collections, or they might be introduced to people in organizations who have the "corporate memory," or they may be asked to interview their grandparents about how family traditions developed.

Technology

The arrangement of events or ideas can easily be done on paper or a blackboard as long as the amount of information to chart is reasonable. But the need to insert events or to track numerous themes across the same time period makes technology extremely valuable. We think of technology in this case as rubberized paper that can expand or contract as we add or erase elements, but still keep everything else in its relative position.

We expect technology to streamline the task students are doing, making it manageable, and even assisting in the production of a timeline ready to be interpreted. The more sophisticated the timeline technology, the more data, ideas, and/or facts can be manipulated. Look for computers and software that make the task easier so that the time for analysis is maximized rather than the time for data gathering or manipulation taking center stage.

For a simple timeline, try the Timeliner created by "Read Write Thinks" at http://www.readwritethink.org/materials/timeline/index.html as a part of the MarcoPolo.org website of technology ideas for teachers. Tom Snyder Productions has created the famous TimeLiner software that will do many simple and very complex timelines.

Critical Information Skills for the Timeline Model

Actively Read, View, Listen
Students will actively and productively read, view, and listen to a variety of resources to extract information relevant to their need.

Today's multimedia world provides a bombardment of fast paced, non-linear information bytes. The implications of the new literacies for the 21st century require us to ensure that all students can decode or "read" all formats, including non-written texts. We must teach students how to interact with all types of media text. They must be able to actively read, view, listen, hunt for key ideas, develop questions, make connections, and reflect on their discoveries. Students need to be not only active, but also critical users of information sources.

Select Relevant Data
Students will identify and select relevant data from a variety of non-fiction resources and record the key points.

At this stage of the process, students are examining sources and applying their active reading, viewing, and listening skills to hunt for those nuggets of information that will help them with their quest. They need to explore the ideas of others before they can start to build their own understanding. Extracting the relevant data, recording it accurately, and keeping it in a safe place until they are ready to process it is the aim of this exercise. Relevance, accuracy, precision, and academic honesty are key elements.

Sort
Students will sort gathered data for specific purposes.

Sorting is an important entry-level analysis skill. Provide students with tactile/concrete sorting experiences before tackling the sorting of data (e.g. sort pictures, books, stamps, etc.). Before students begin to sort, clear purpose and criteria must be established.

Note Making
Students will develop note making skills and a variety of strategies for organizing the selected data.

Once students have identified and gathered the best sources of information for their inquiry, they must prepare to collect the data they need to answer their inquiry question. Students now need to be taught how to identify the information they need and to develop a variety of strategies for keeping all this information organized. When students are taking notes from their sources, they are already starting to analyze their data.

Identify and Investigate Patterns and Trends
Students will identify and investigate patterns and trends related to their inquiries.

This skill is a pre-requisite for making predictions. Students will need lots of modeling and practice with identifying and investigating patterns and trends. Start with familiar patterns of similar ideas or things. When patterns are identified, look for trends over time. Students should learn to look for patterns and trends in all investigations. This skill has many specific applications (e.g. media studies, mathematics, weather, population growth, investigation of economic issues like supply and demand, trade, investment, marketing etc).

Examples of the Timeline Model

Unit 29: Growing Up   Gr. 1–3

How much have I changed since I was a baby?

Problem

During the "all about me" unit, students will examine how they have changed over time. Review the concept of change through pictures and discussion. Chart some changes suggested by the children. Introduce the notion of growing up with the popular story by Robert Munsch, *Love You Forever.*

Gathering Facts

Ask students, "What changes occurred in this story?" Sort the changes on a T-chart (Mother's changes, boy's changes) as students recall. Review the story and illustrations as necessary. Have students work with a partner or a small group. Ask students to choose a change in the boy's or the mother's life and prepare a drawing to illustrate the change. Provide students with drawing materials and a square piece of sturdy paper. Ensure that all major changes have an illustrator.

Creating Timeline

When the illustrations are complete, pin them to a long cord across the classroom, like clothes on a clothesline. This will create a visual timeline of the boy's and the mother's life.

Analysis

Invite students to retell the story. Discuss feelings about growing up from all perspectives: the boy's, the mother's and the listener's.

So What?

Students can create a visual timeline of their own growing up years. Send home a letter to families explaining the project. Have each student interview family members to discover important events in their lives (e.g. birth, sitting up, first tooth, swimming lessons, birthdays, parties etc.). Provide students with several copies of the organizer *Growing Up.* Students illustrate the important events in their lives and create a personal pictorial time line.

Unit 30: The Eye of the Storm   Gr. 9–12

How have events related to Iraq kept the world in a state of turmoil over the last quarter century?

Problem

Modern History classes are grappling with the causes and effects of war in Iraq. First they will gather facts about the history of the turmoil. Next they will analyze the facts by creating a timeline that will give students a concrete picture of events and the interrelationship of these events as they unfold.

Gathering Facts

Group students and assign a focus country or organization for fact gathering (e.g. Group A: Iraq, Group B: USA, Group C: Britain, Group D: United Nations, Group E: France, Group F: Russia). Remind students to use several sources and to validate and document them. Keep accurate, organized notes.

Placement on the Timeline

The nature and volume of all the data from the main stakeholders in this world crisis will require students to experiment with the best way to organize. They will need to back up each event with the pertinent background information. The best way to handle such a vast project is probably electronically, by creating an interactive webpage. For specific help with designing a timeline, see *Tips for Terrific Timelines* and the *Timeline Rubric.*

Analysis

Once all the data from all groups is organized in an effective timeline, reassemble the students into groups, ABCDEF. Review the focus question and charge groups with the task of looking for relationships, patterns, discrepancies, surprises, etc. from the collective timeline data.

So What?

Students use this exploratory experience to provide background for a creating a thesis statement for their term paper.

Unit 31: Clockwork   Gr. 1–4

How do clocks help us?

Gathering Facts
Have students look through old magazines and catalogues for pictures of clocks and other timepieces. Cut out, sort, and categorize.

Introduce engaging question. Arrange students in triads with another classmate and an older learning buddy. The task is to interview a school community member and record what they do during the school day. Provide triads with a Clockwork *Time Log* organizer and the interview questions. Use a different color for each group. Groups proceed to interview an assigned school member (e.g. principal, teacher, secretary, caretaker, parent, library media specialist, ed assistants, students etc). They record activity for each time slot from 8:00 am to 4:00 pm.

Creating Timeline
Have each group cut up their time log chart and place information on a large circular time-line with a clock face in the middle.

Analyze
Ask each group to share the "day story" of their survey subject, hour by hour, and then pose some analysis questions. E.g. Are there any times when several people are doing the same thing? Do the things one person does affect others? What might happen if someone didn't have a clock? Record findings on a chart.

So What?
Restate the engaging question. Chart student responses.

Ask students to draw pictures and record, with assistance when necessary, several ways that clocks help them and their school community. In small groups have students share their findings.

Gathering Evidence of Understanding
- students can identify the criteria they used to sort and categorize
- data is complete and accurate
- drawings reflect the ways clocks help
- students are able to articulate a number of roles clocks play in daily life

Info Skills
- actively read, view, listen
- select relevant data
- sort
- note making
- identify and investigate patterns and trends

Reflect, Rethink, Redesign
- Were students able to find enough variety in timepieces in the materials I provided?
- Did the interview questions glean the quality and quantity of information we needed?
- Did the analysis questions lead the students to make insightful observations?
- Did any students challenge the assumption of the engaging question? Were they able to support their position?
- How could I streamline this process so it would be more successful next time?
- How did the timeline help students understand the value of clocks in daily life?

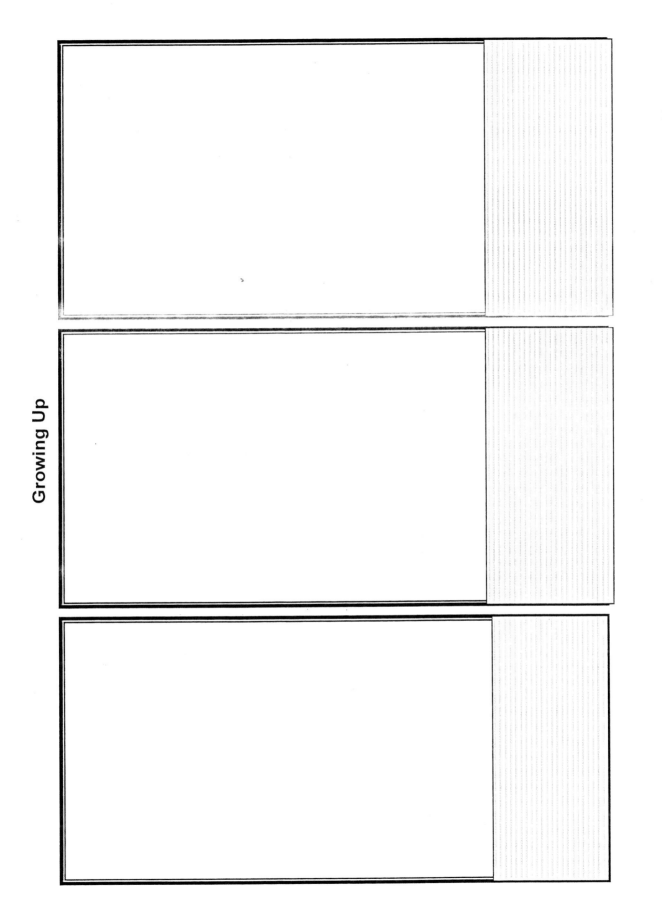

Growing Up

Tips for Terrific Timelines

1. How can a timeline help me?

▶ Timelines show small snapshots of events and help us see change over time.

▶ Timelines make it easier to see causes and effects.

▶ Timelines make it easier to see relationships and make connections.

2. What do I want people to learn from my timeline?

3. How can I make a timeline that will convey my message?

▶ List all the items/events you think you want to include on your timeline.

▶ Sort your items/events by putting them in chronological order.

▶ Check to be sure you have included all the important, significant items/events.

▶ Check to see if all the items/events you have chosen to be *entries* are related to your purpose.

▶ Sort your *entries* again if necessary.

▶ Look carefully at the number of *entries* you have and think about the length of time they span.

▶ Think about how time should be broken down. Experiment with time *increments* (e.g. centuries, decades, years, months, days, hours, minutes).

▶ Decide on the most effective *increment* for your purpose, and use that as your *scale*.

▶ Decide on the time for beginning and ending your line.

▶ Select a way of marking the increments on your line.

▶ Decide on where to place the entries: above the line, below the line, alternating...

▶ Think about the use of graphics and color to make your line more effective and attractive.

▶ Be sure to keep it clear and uncluttered.

4. Is this a logical application for commercial timeline software?

Timeline Rubric

Level	Content	Scale	Citations	Presentation
Level Four	- entries show careful selection for relevance and impact (connections, relationships and patterns are evident) - all data is accurate	- scale selected is very effective for topic - increments marked are clear and effective and are accurately placed - placement of entries on the line is consistent and accurate - intent of timeline is clear to viewer (connections, relationships and patterns are very obvious)	- all sources accurately referenced	- visually appealing - appropriate and effective graphics and use of color - easily legible and well-balanced
Level Three	- entries are adequate, on topic - data is accurate	- scale selected is appropriate for topic - increments are well marked and accurately placed - placement of entries on the line is consistent and accurate - intent of timeline is clear to viewer (connections, relationships and patterns can be identified)	- all sources accurately referenced	- attractive - graphics related to subject. and use of color is effective - clear and uncluttered
Level Two	- some important data is missing - some inaccuracies in data	- scale selected is poor - increments are poorly marked and sometimes inaccurate - some entries are out of sequence - intent is difficult to discern	- most sources accurately referenced	- little attempt to embellish - ineffective use of color and graphics - unclear and/or cluttered
Level One	- data poorly selected in terms of importance, relevance and impact - many inaccuracies in data	- scale is inappropriate or not apparent - increments inaccurate and or ineffectively marked - many entries not in sequence - no indication of intent	- few sources accurately referenced	- no visible attempt to make line attractive - little or no use of graphics and/or color - messy and difficult to read

Clock Work Time Log

Time	Activity	Who
8:00-8:30		
8:30-9:00		
9:00-9:30		
9:30-10:00		
10:00-10:30		
10:30-11:00		
11:00-11:30		
11:30-12:00		
12:00-12:30		
12:30-1:00		
1:00-1:30		
1:30-2:00		
2:00-2:30		
2:30-3:00		
3:00-3:30		
3:30-4:00		

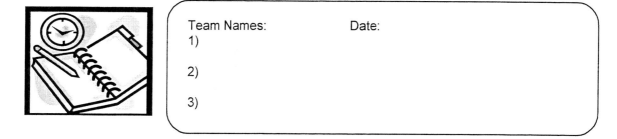

Team Names: Date:
1)

2)

3)

History & Mystery Model

History & Mystery Model

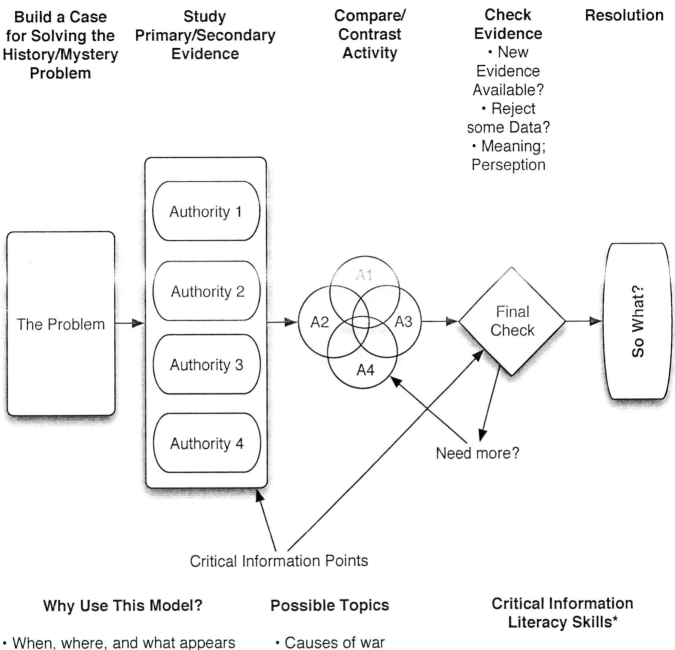

| Build a Case for Solving the History/Mystery Problem | Study Primary/Secondary Evidence | Compare/ Contrast Activity | Check Evidence • New Evidence Available? • Reject some Data? • Meaning; Perseption | Resolution |

The Problem

Authority 1

Authority 2

Authority 3

Authority 4

A1
A2
A3
A4

Final Check

So What?

Need more?

Critical Information Points

Why Use This Model?

• When, where, and what appears to have happened?
• What really happened?
• Why did it happen?
• What could have prevented it from happening?
• What can we learn based on what happened and why?

Possible Topics

• Causes of war
• Change in government
• Natural catastropies
• Advances in technology
• Influence of artists/ authors
• Development of art forms and genres

Critical Information Literacy Skills*

• Select Relevant Data, K&Z p. 62
• Sort, K&Z p. 94
• Determining Fact, K&Z p. 66
• Compare, K&Z p. 98
• Make Connections, K&Z p. 116

* Koechlin, Carol and Sandi Zwaan. *Build Your Own Information Literate School.* Hi Willow, 2003.

Notes on the History & Mystery Model

Solving a mystery in any discipline or finding out what happened in a particular time period is a common learning experience and part of everyday life. Why do ships seem to disappear in the Bermuda Triangle? Is the *DaVinci Code* accurate in its portrayal of the life of Jesus? What are the origins of the compass rose and superstitions about Friday the 13th in that book? Conspiracy theorists often reinterpret an event or a part of history to support varying notions of what or why something happened. For example, did Roosevelt know about the attack on Pearl Harbor before it happened?

To solve a mystery or judge what really happened, quality information sources play a central role. The History & Mystery Model provides both an opportunity to teach the difference between an original and a secondary source, and to gather the best evidence before a judgment or a conclusion is made. Bias, popular explanations, and plain misconceptions can often be changed in the light of accurate evidence. In the course of researching a decade, trying to figure out how the pyramids were built, why the dinosaurs disappeared, or how crop circles were created, the teacher and librarian will want to plan what resources are needed for the various types of evidence to be explored. The entire Internet is probably not the best starting place unless students are carefully taught to evaluate the quality of information they will encounter.

Once evidence is found, judged as accurate, and allowed into formal consideration, students will no doubt have varying facts and opinions of what happened. Again, this will present the perfect opportunity to teach sound reasoning and proper analysis. We should remind our students that our knowledge of any event is partial, and our conclusions may change if and when new and more accurate evidence appears.

Technology

The Internet has become a wonderful tool for the exploration of original documents and resources. Museums and archives throughout the world are scanning original resources and making them available on the Web. The Library of Congress, the British Museum, the Smithsonian Institution, the United States Holocaust Memorial Museum, Ellis Island's American Family Immigration History Center, Schomburg Center for Research in Black Culture, and American Presidential libraries are but a few examples of vast resources available. Librarians will need to provide instruction on searching and citing such collections or download specific examples of documents, if time is at a premium.

The Internet also contains many spurious and non-authentic reproductions of primary materials used for propaganda or outright misinformation. Students, teachers, and librarians will have to collaborate to judge the authenticity and relevance of such sources.

Many original resources can be cut and pasted into reports using image-editing programs such as Photoshop to touch up or modify original documents to suit their purposes. For example, they could insert their own face into a group picture of President Truman shaking their hand or they could put an original document on one side of a page and translate or comment on that document in the margins.

Critical Information Skills for History and Mystery Model

Select Relevant Data
Students will identify and select relevant data from a variety of non-fiction resources and record the key points.

At this stage of the process, students are examining sources and applying their active reading, viewing and listening skills to hunt for those nuggets of information that will help them with their quest. They need to explore the ideas of others before they can start to build their own understanding. Extracting the relevant data, recording it accurately, and keeping it in a safe place until they are ready to process it is the aim of this exercise. Relevance, accuracy, precision, and academic honesty are key elements.

Sort
Students will sort gathered data for specific purposes

Sorting is an important entry-level analysis skill. Provide students with tactile/concrete sorting experiences before tackling the sorting of data (e.g. sort pictures, books, and stamps). Before students begin to sort, clear purpose and criteria must be established.

Determining Fact
Students will compare information sources to determine what is fact.

As students work with a variety of resources, they are often frustrated or confused by the conflicting information they detect. They need practice discovering and confirming factual information. Young students learn to sort fact from fiction and progress to sorting facts from opinions. Ultimately, they make personal links or reactions to the information they select.

Compare
Students will make comparisons to discover relationships in gathered data.

Making comparisons is actually a complex process. Students must first of all determine exactly what is being compared and why, then decide which aspects of the items they will examine for the purposes of comparison. Consequently, they need at least two bodies of information and pre-determined criteria to help sort the points of comparison. Once sorted, they need to determine what is similar and what is different.

Make Connections
Students will work with information to make connections.

Just as we help students make meaning when reading fiction, we need to structure similar activities to help them build connections as they read, view, and listen to non-fiction text. There are many "connection building" strategies we can teach to help students understand content. When we suggest that students make connections, we want them to make links to what they already know: what they know about the topic, what they know about reading (viewing/listening) strategies, what they know about webbing/mapping, and how this new content fits into their personal experiences.

Examples of the History and Mystery Model
Unit 32: The Unsinkable Ship   Gr. 6–8

Problem

The Titanic was billed as the most luxurious and safest ship on the sea. Was the claim that it was "unsinkable" justified?

Study of Primary and Secondary Evidence

Using an organizer, students take careful notes of claims, structure of the ship, evidence to support claims made regarding safety (noting the author), special safety features, flaws discovered, investigation reports.

Authority 1 copies of archival documents

Authority 2 print books

Authority 3 video (Secrets of the Titanic - National Geographic)

Authority 4 specific websites

Compare/Contrast Activity

Groups of four students meet to compare notes. Highlight similarities with one color, differences or discrepancies with another. Students make a case for or against the claim.

Evidence Check

Students revisit their authorities to re-check discrepancies. They consult more authorities, to validate the source. They research new perspectives and come to consensus about the claim.

So What?

This activity can be the spark for further independent study or a myriad of creative extensions, such as writing a short fictional story based on facts about the Titanic.

Unit 33: Mayday   Gr. 9–12

Problem

Although flying today on a major commercial airliner is a very safe mode of transportation, things can go wrong, and when they do, many lives are lost. It is crucial to discover exactly what went wrong so pilots and engineers can make sure it never happens again. This often requires a great deal of detective work and analysis. *Who is involved in the investigation? How do they go about tracing the cause of the accident when everything is destroyed?*

Study Primary and Secondary Evidence

Decide on four or five major air crashes, depending on how many groups you want. Assign each group an air disaster to investigate. Instruct each group to examine all the data they can recover about the disaster, especially the efforts made to piece together the most probable scenario of what happened. Source some of the many texts available on air crash detective work. Specific web resources will be invaluable, as will periodical databases, news footage and documentaries (such as The Investigation of Swiss Air 111,The Nature of Things, CBC).

Authority # 1	03/09/1998	Nova Scotia, Canada	MD -11	Swiss Air
Authority # 2	25/07/2000	Paris, France	Concorde	Air France
Authority # 3	11/12/2001	Belle Harbor, USA	Airbus A300	American Airlines
Authority #4	31/10/ 1999	Nantucket, USA	767	Egypt Air

Compare/Contrast Activity

JigSaw groups of students meet to compare notes. (See Concept JigSaw Model.) Students highlight similarities with one color differences or discrepancies with another. Review the guiding questions and develop a flow chart to represent the usual steps taken and the resulting implications of the investigations.

Evidence Check

Students revisit their authorities to re-check discrepancies. They consult more authorities making sure to validate the source. They research any new angles and methods they have discovered and come to a consensus regarding their flow chart.

So What?

Students investigate the variety of career paths that could lead to jobs in the investigation of aircraft crashes and other similar events.

Unit 34: Mayan Mysteries   Gr. 4–6

What evidence can you find to prove that the ancient Mayans were a highly skilled civilization?

Problem
Read aloud a Mayan myth and then provide the students with other Mayan myths to read independently. Discuss in small groups. Introduce the guiding question.

Study Primary and Secondary Evidence
Assign groups a selected set of resources rich with information on Mayan culture. E.g. Authorities: 1. on-line encyclopedia, 2. videos, 3. non-fiction books, 4. book-marked websites. Students use *Mysteries of Mayan Culture* to record their evidence and their explanation of why or how it demonstrates superior skills. E.g. Evidence: Mayan glyphs, Support: hard to read and can be read from left to right, top to bottom, or bottom to top.

Compare/Contrast
Have two groups meet and present their findings. They should look for similarities, differences, and missing or conflicting information. They should help each other to identify gaps in the evidence or other flaws in conclusions. Groups confirm with each other the items to be declared "evidence of a highly skilled civilization."

Check Evidence
Students should return to their sources if they feel they have not been able to build a convincing amount of supporting evidence. They may also need to revisit sources to confirm ideas.

So What?
Each group prepares a presentation to share their documented evidence found to support the belief that the Mayans were a highly skilled civilization. Students may illustrate their findings with drawings, maps and charts, and prepare to present their findings.

Students could compare their evidence with the sophistication of similar items from another ancient culture they have studied.

Gathering Evidence of Understanding
- a variety of examples that demonstrate the skill of the Mayans
- logical connections between examples and supporting evidence
- searches for information were effective
- individuals and groups supported each other

Info Skills
- select relevant data
- sort
- compare
- classify
- make connections

Reflect, Rethink, Redesign
- Are there resources to address all levels of student skills?
- Are there students who require assistance finding support for their examples? Would some prompts help?
- Is the support they found adequate? Are they able to make the connections between the examples and what it is about them that demonstrates superior skill?
- Did group members encourage each other as they worked together?
- Do students need some ideas/prompts for identifying supporting details?
- Have groups established who or how they will present their evidence?

Mysteries of Mayan Culture

Look for clues that the Mayans were very skilled people.
List the examples in the **Evidence** column.
Ask yourself why this clue shows they were highly skilled.
List your proof in the **Support** column.

Evidence	Support

Take a Position Model

Take a Position Model

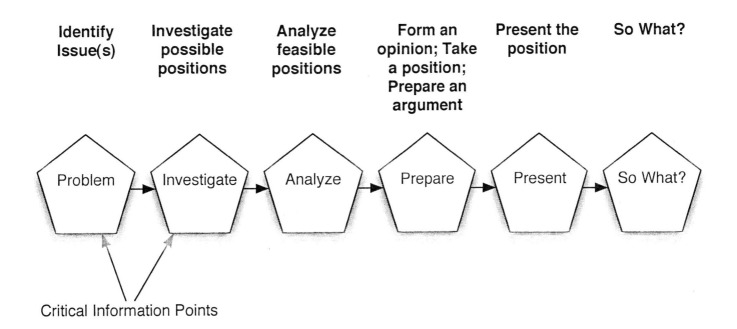

Identify Issue(s) | Investigate possible positions | Analyze feasible positions | Form an opinion; Take a position; Prepare an argument | Present the position | So What?

Problem → Investigate → Analyze → Prepare → Present → So What?

Critical Information Points

Why This Model?

• Learn to take positions on sound ideas rather than on snap judgments
• Learn how to understand ideas much different than your own
• Develop critical analysis skills in the face of propaganda
• Build empathy for all positions, even as you take a stand
• Learn to articulate and defend a position taken
• Build the skills for living and participating in a democratic society

Sample Topics

• Political issues
• Controversial science problems
• Historical issues
• Moral issues
• Community problems
• School problems
• Literary critical issues

Sample Products:

• Position paper
• Persuasive speech
• Video presentation
• PowerPoint presentation
• Debate
• Panel discussion
• Switch positions, then present
• Action plan

Critical Information Literacy Skills*

• Actively Read, View, and Listen, K&Z p. 45
• Select Relevant Data, K&Z p. 62
• Determine Fact, K&Z p. 66
• Understanding Perspective, K&Z p. 136
• Share and Use, K&Z p. 155

* Koechlin, Carol and Sandi Zwaan. *Build Your Own Information Literate School.* Hi Willow, 2003

Notes on Take a Position Model

Sometimes we may take a position on an issue in the heat of debate, just to be argumentative, or for the equally spurious reason that we like someone who holds the same opinion. We should not model this kind of haphazard position-taking for our students. Instead we should coach our students in a much more difficult and genuine learning experience by asking them to take an informed position based on the best information available about the issue at hand. The Take a Position Model asks that students to go beyond the teacher, textbook, or in-class debate to thoroughly investigate an issue, analyze the information found, compare and contrast what they find, make a serious analysis, synthesize the evidence, and then take a defensible position.

We rely on "experts" from every walk of life to build informed opinions, judgments, and public policy based on extensive investigations and sound analysis, rather than on whim. Students need to be exposed to projects that require deep analysis and result in informed opinions. Such learning experiences will rely heavily on quality information systems to reveal quality spokespersons on each side of the issue. If students are novices at analyzing such information, they will need a great deal of help in sorting out ideas, judging positions, classifying voices, and making judgments through reason rather than on passion.

To sort through the various voices on an issue, students might be introduced to the "Take a Positions Worksheet." Both individuals and groups can learn to classify a writer or speaker along a continuum, being for or against an issue. For novices, information that is polarized one way or another will be the easiest to deal with. The writer is either for or against junk food in the school. More sophisticated students can handle articles, authors, or speakers who are wishy-washy or who encrypt their message so that placement on a position continuum is difficult. Reading these types of authors or listening to their speeches will be a major test in reading comprehension, listening skills, as well as the ability to group this speaker with others or place the author along the continuum. To assist in this, the Take a Position Line handout has been created for the teacher demonstrating how various opinions can be charted on the board or on some kind of chart, created by either the students or the teacher. This line is on p. 140.

Taking an informed position is the perfect time to analyze: Who is saying what to me for what reasons and with what expected result? It is a perfect time to discuss propaganda: what it is, how it works, and how it is used in our daily lives, from politics to advertising.

Technology

Good search engines of databases, the Web, and the invisible Web, will allow students to uncover many of the sources they will need on most any issue. Tracking articles, quotes, and excerpts with complete citations will help the student know who said what, when, and where. A good tracking system will allow the student to concentrate on analysis, grouping, synthesis, and drawing conclusions. Technology will also be useful in presenting the various sides of an issue so that audiences can clearly see the results of the research and the expertise used in analysis.

Take a Position Worksheet
Position Line

Create a Position Line using string, yarn or tape along the length or width of the classroom. Identify the polarity at either end of the line.

As students research an issue, instruct them to think about where candidates, stakeholders, journalists, & lobbyists, would sit on the Position Line.

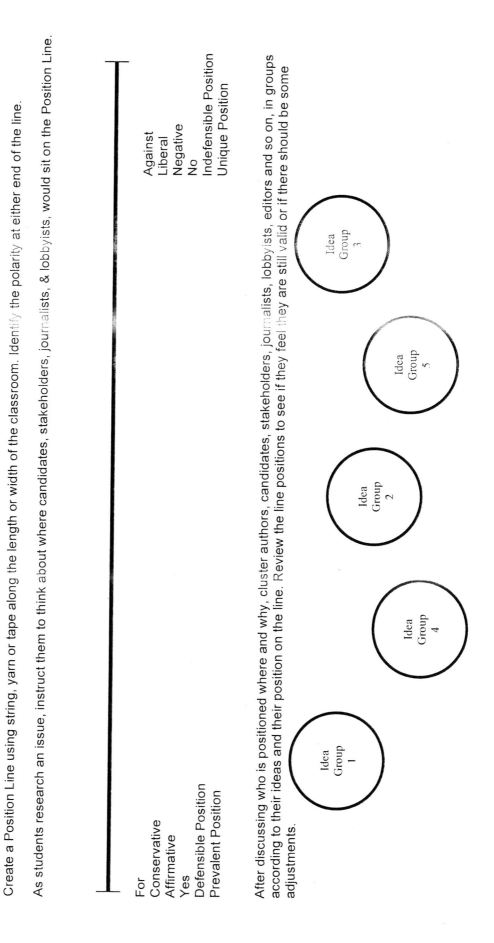

For	Against
Conservative	Liberal
Affirmative	Negative
Yes	No
Defensible Position	Indefensible Position
Prevalent Position	Unique Position

After discussing who is positioned where and why, cluster authors, candidates, stakeholders, journalists, lobbyists, editors and so on, in groups according to their ideas and their position on the line. Review the line positions to see if they feel they are still valid or if there should be some adjustments.

Critical Information Skills for Take a Position Model

Actively Read, View, Listen
Students will actively and productively read, view, and listen to a variety of resources to extract information relevant to their need.

Today's multimedia world provides a bombardment of fast paced, non-linear information bytes. The implications of the new literacies for the 21st century require us to ensure that all students can decode or "read" all formats including non-written texts. We must teach students how to interact with all types of media text. They must be able to actively read, view, listen, hunt for key ideas, develop questions, make connections, and reflect on their discoveries. Students need to be not only active but also critical users of information sources.

Select Relevant Data
Students will identify and select relevant data from a variety of non-fiction resources and record the key points.

At this stage of the process, students are examining sources and applying their active reading, viewing, and listening skills to hunt for those nuggets of information that will help them with their quest. They need to explore the ideas of others before they can start to build their own understanding. Extracting the relevant data, recording it accurately, and keeping it in a safe place until they are ready to process it is the aim of this exercise. Relevance, accuracy, precision, and academic honesty are key elements.

Determining Fact
Students will compare information sources to determine what is fact.

As students work with a variety of resources, they are often frustrated or confused by the conflicting information they detect. They need practice discovering and confirming factual information. Young students learn to sort fact from fiction and progress to sorting facts from opinions. Ultimately, they make personal links or reactions to the information they select.

Understanding Perspective
Students will analyze information to identify and examine perspective in order to gain understanding.

Perspective is powerful when it comes to information. The ability to examine a text and determine perspective is an important skill for working with complex issues. To be able to gain understanding through perspective requires a high level of critical thinking. Helping students gain perspective empowers them to be alert and to think critically about accepted or common theories.

Share and Use
Students will share and use their new knowledge and insight.

This skill requires lots of carefully planned teaching and guidance. Ultimately we want students to select format, create, and present independently. In preparation for this independence, we need to teach the process of creating a variety of types of presentation. Often students put so much emphasis on the product/presentation that process and new knowledge are lost in glitzy appearance and pizzazz. We can counteract this by clearly including specifics regarding content and process skills in the evaluation outline that we share with students before they begin.

Examples of the Take a Position Model

Unit 35: Playground Cleanup   Gr. 2–3

Problem: *Is our playground clean and safe?*

Investigate: Provide students with amateur sleuth equipment (e.g. clipboards and a camera). Take them on a playground walk and instruct them to sketch and take notes of things they really like as well as evidence of any litter and unsafe conditions in their playground.

Analyze: On a large bulletin board map of the playground, have students place their sketches, photographs, and notes on the map appropriately. Ask students to think about what they like and don't like about their playground. Create a T-Chart on which to sort and record student thoughts.

Prepare: Provide each student with a set of happy and sad face stickers. Pose the engaging question again, "Is our playground clean and safe?" Ask students to place a happy face sticker on their hand if they are happy with their playground the way it is, and a sad face sticker on their hand if they think their playground should be cleaner and safer. Have students meet in like groups and prepare materials to present their positions (e.g. stories, poems, pictures, lists, and letters).

Present: Students share their position pieces with other classes, the principal, chief caretaker, parent council...

So What? Students who are positive about their playground can meet to plan ways to make better use of the facility, and those who want to see improvements can meet to plan how to get their message heard and some action taken.

Unit 36: Book Club Choices   Gr. 4–6

Problem: *Which book titles are suitable for club discussion this year?*

Investigate: Each student in your book club reads several current titles of their choice.

Analyze: With the group, develop criteria for analyzing and evaluating titles for this year's club reading list (e.g. good character development, universal theme, interesting style, and special technique).

Prepare: Each student selects the book they think they and others in their club would enjoy discussing and prepares a short summary and rationale for their book club choice.

Present: The selected title summaries are compiled and posted to members of the club. Each member selects the 5-6 titles they would like to discuss this year. From this survey, the titles are selected for the book list.

So What? Students who have already read the book can meet to develop a few discussion questions. Students who have read none of the titles on the list can develop some pre-reading questions based on the summary information they have.

Note: This strategy could work well for either face-to-face or virtual book clubs. Check out these sites for virtual formats or start your own.

- Book Rap: http://rite.ed.qut.edu.au/old_oz-teachernet/projects/book-rap/
- Book BackChat: http://english.unitecnology.ac.nz/bookchat/about.html
- Teenreads: http://www.teenreads.com/

Unit 37: Candidate Candor   Gr. 7–12

Where do the candidates stand on global warming, stem cell research, interest free student loans...?

Investigate
Present and discuss the issue/engaging question. Provide students with ample activities to explore the topic so that they are able to identify the key interest groups. Divide the class so that an equal number is assigned to investigate each of the key candidates or interest groups to discover their position and their rationale for that position. Provide each student with a copy of *Prevailing Positions* worksheet to record their findings.

Create a long position line across the width of the classroom, on the chalkboard if possible, identifying only the ends: one as positive, fully supports; the other as negative, totally opposes. See *Take a Position Teacher Reference*.

Analyze
Group students according to the candidate/interest group they represent. Have groups meet to discuss their findings, using their completed organizers, and to determine where they believe their candidate/group should be positioned on the line.

Prepare
Provide each group with an index card to label and affix to the position line in the appropriate location.

Present
Have a representative from each group place their card on the position line and explain the opinion of their candidate/group and the rationale for their stance.

So What?
Restate the engaging question. As a group, study the completed position line and look for clusters and spaces between cards. Note which groups/candidates are where and so on. Ask students what they can determine from the line. In a personal response journal, have students respond to the following questions. How do you feel about what you see? What new questions do you have? Where would you place yourself on the position line?

Gathering Evidence of Understanding

o   efficacy of student exploration of the topic will indicate accurate identification of the issues and positions.
o   groups are able to agree about their stakeholders' position on the line.
o   individual students are able to answer response journal questions and justify their answers.

Info Skills:
o   explore a topic
o   actively read, view and listen
o   select relevant data
o   understand perspective - identify, & consider
o   interpret and infer
o   reflect, transfer and apply

Reflect, Rethink, Redesign
o   Were the resources varied and relevant enough to allow students to discover the stakeholders and identify their issues and positions?
o   Are students able to independently assign and carry out group roles? If not, what can I do to rectify the situation?
o   How did groups reach consensus regarding the position of their card on the line? Would it help others to hear how the successful groups did this?
o   Where else could this strategy be applied to help students develop understanding of issues in curriculum topics?
o   What are the indicators that this exercise affected student opinion? Do students realize the role this process played in their development of personal understanding?
o   How can I ensure that they see how valuable this is and how they can use it other situations?

Unit 38: Pesky Propositions   Gr. 9–12

What is your position on the proposed statewide ban on the use of pesticides and herbicides?

Investigate

Provide a variety of exploration activities to give the students an overview of the topic and to help them identify the stakeholders. After the exploration activities, convene as a group and make a master list of the key stakeholders in this issue. Divide the class into groups and assign each a stakeholder role. Have groups consider how use or non-use of these substances would affect them. They are to investigate and record both positive and negative aspects of the use of herbicides and pesticides domestically and commercially from the stakeholder's perspective. As with any issue, it will be very important to sort out the facts from opinions and propaganda.

Analyze

Provide students with individual copies of *Linking to Fact and Opinion* so they can record, sort, and analyze as they go along, completing the My Questions and My Reactions columns after data gathering of the stakeholder role. Ask students to share and discuss individual findings in their groups and then identify key facts. As a group, create a common list of the positive and negative facts that pertain to their perspective.

Prepare

Students use these lists as the basis for discussion while they share their thoughts and reactions. Have students use the *Prevailing Positions* worksheet to create a Position Paper press release for their group. Select representatives to speak for the groups at the press conference.

Present

Schedule a press conference and distribute copies of the stakeholders' Position Papers in advance so others can read them and be prepared to question them at the conference.

So What?

Restate the question to the class and have individual students use the *Understand Perspectives* work sheet to consider all the stake holders and then express their own personal positions.

Gathering Evidence of Understanding

- Students were able to identify all important stakeholders and positive and negative factors.
- Facts were identified and analyzed.
- Stakeholder positions were clearly articulated and defended.
- Individual positions were identified and explained.

Info Skills:

- explore a topic
- actively read, view and listen
- select relevant data
- understand perspective
- synthesize - draw conclusions, gain perspective, and form an opinion
- take and defend a position

Reflect, Rethink, Redesign

- Did the exploration activities expose students to the relevant stakeholders and their concerns?
- Were there adequate resources at appropriate levels to meet all student needs?
- Were students able to assign and follow group roles for chair, recorder, publisher, presenter...? If not, what must I do to prepare them to do this independently next time?
- Were students able to engage in the stakeholder role effectively? Who couldn't? How could I help?
- Did any of the groups investigate actions and reactions to this issue in other states and countries?
- Do they realize that other positions are valid to the group that holds them?
- Did they show empathy for other stakeholders' positions as they formed their own opinion and decided on a personal position?
- Is there student interest in taking some further action?
- What might I do to facilitate further action?

Prevailing Positions

Topic

Important facts

-

-

-

-

Stakeholder

Issue Impact on stakeholder	Issue Impact on stakeholder
Issue Impact on stakeholder	Issue Impact on stakeholder

Having considered all the issues and their impact, the perspective of this group is...

Because...

Linking to Facts and Opinions

Name: ....

Topic: ....

Facts				Opinions	
	My Questions				My Reactions
Perhaps...					

Reprinted with permission from *InfoTasks for Successful Learning*, Pembroke Publishers 2001

146   Take a Position Model

Understand Perspectives

Issue

Just the facts
- - - -

Stakeholders

-------------------' perspective Rationale
-------------------' perspective Rationale

-------------------' perspective Rationale
-------------------' perspective Rationale

Having considered all the perspectives and the reasons for them, my perspective of this issue is...

Because...

The Re-Create Model

The Re-Create Model

| Select event, issue, time period piece | Explore event/ drama | Research every possible aspect to ensure authenticity | Select Format and Construct | Perform as:
• Drama
• Event
• Diary
• Newspaper
• Picture
• Painting
• Story | Big Picture |

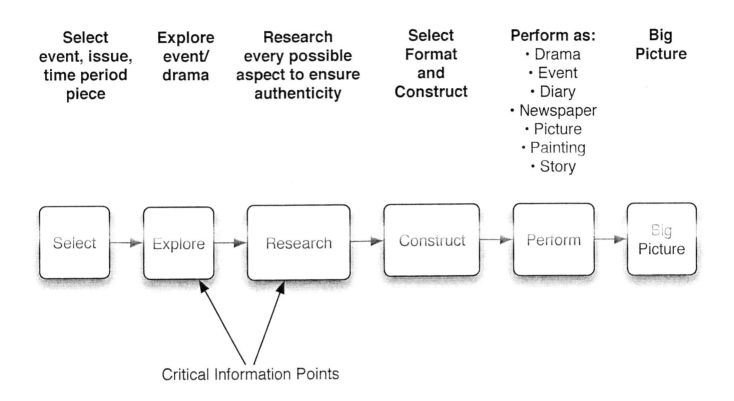

Critical Information Points

Why This Model?

• Why do things, seemingly strange, make sense in context?
• What kinds of persons contribute or distract while a major event is unfolding?
• What can we learn from the unfolding of major events?
• How does excellence in the reconstruction of an event help in the understanding of that event?
• Can we develop empathy for people in their time and place?
• Can we walk in someone else's shoes?
• So we judge the difference between fiction and realistic fiction.

Possible Topics:

• Life in a place/time
• Historical event
• Perform a play that requires authenticity
• Pioneer life
• Slavery
• Interview an historical personality

Critical Information Literacy Skills*

• Use Primary Sources, K&Z p. 46
• Read Pictures, K&Z p. 70
• Make Connections, K&Z p. 116
• Interpret, Infer, Predict, K&Z p. 130
• Respond to Text, K&Z p. 112
• Impact, K&Z p. 124

* Koechlin, Carol and Sandi Zwaan. *Build Your Own Information Literate School*. Hi Willow, 2003.

Notes for the Re-Create Model

Through the magic of television or video, students can see re-enactments of events or time periods, or experience current events in real time. Students may watch the procession of Ronald Regan's casket through the streets of Washington D.C., see an actual debate in Congress, or see Roosevelt's Dec. 7th speech to the nation about Pearl Harbor.

Documentaries are supposed to recreate events faithfully and Hollywood movies often attempt to be historically accurate for a time and place such as in *High Noon* (a western) or *Apollo 13* (a re-creation of the near Apollo 13 disaster).

Students may be challenged to re-create an event, put on a play, or do a readers theatre where props, costumes, backdrops or other elements are to be as accurate as possible. To do so, solid research in a variety of information sources will provide the basic clues, plans, or ideas for re-creation. Even if students are illustrating reports, they can be held responsible for accurate pictures of the past. Points might be deducted for a picture of French royalty in costume when the topic of the report is French peasant life. Children have also been known to take a dinosaur book to the librarian to point out inaccuracies by artists who put wrong heads on wrong bodies. Those same children might object to fluorescent green, purple, or black dinosaurs, until they discover that no one has been able to determine the actual color of any of the dinosaurs from extant bones in digs.

Whether children are trying to re-create the first Thanksgiving holiday or deliver the Martin Luther King speech, the environment and the period costume and food will enhance the experience both for the actor and the audience. Often the re-creation of an event provides perspective on, empathy for, and deep understanding of that event. In one elementary school, students lived for a week in a model of a 19th century pioneer house reconstructed in the basement of the school—wearing what those people wore, eating what they ate, and trying to survive without television or video games. These students spent a great deal of time learning about real life on the plains in early Illinois before they were allowed in their model house. Teachers and librarians wanted as much authenticity as possible so that each child could appreciate those people who have paved the way for modern living.

Bias and cultural issues must be researched carefully before presentation. Should this Indian chief wear a long feathered headdress and brandish a tomahawk? Could a Hmong villager wear a pair of denim jeans? What kind of hat did Lincoln wear when he delivered the Gettysburg Address? Did he use a microphone? A great deal of significance can be lost and misconceptions go unchallenged when shoddy or insufficient research precedes a presentation.

Technology

Using PhotoShop (or other comparable photographic software) or iMovie, students can add authenticity to a street scene by removing telephone poles, wires, and adding or subtracting various elements from a number of photos, creating a single work that would represent a time period. Students can also superimpose their faces or their person into a scene so they are "at the battle" and can then respond to writing prompts as if they were there.

Using video editing tools, students can perform and record easily what would have taken weeks and months just a few years ago. They might show short clips from documentaries as a part of a larger project. Or they can create their own footage or stage events using such programs as iMovie (for the Mac) or Visual Communicator (for the PC).

Challenge students to learn the techniques of adding authenticity based on their research. The technology will often drive the motivation to work at the research until the product is as authentic as possible, given the normal time constraints. Design software with Internet access will provide a gateway to millions of photographs, line drawings, patterns, cut-away models, authentic photos of times, places, people, architecture, and a whole host of topical visual as well as print descriptions. There is little excuse not to dress up a production, a report, or any type of production with an authentic flavor.

There are a number of authentic re-creations of events, cultures, and time periods. One example is the PBS Colonial Villiage at:
http://www.pbs.org/whet/colonialhouse/history/panoramas.html

 Here, children can explore a colonial village in virtual space as if they were touring it themselves and can look around, study something in detail, or get a picture of the entire village.

Other sources of great re-creations include the National Film Board of Canada, The Discovery Channel, The History Channel, The Smithsonian Institution web portal, the National Archives of Canada, and the CBC Archives.

Research

"Creating a story to be acted out by themselves and others can improve students' language and skills, self concept, peer relationships, and creativity."[1] The re-create model requires in addition that students be as authentic as possible to increase their understanding as well as the benefits that creative drama provide.

---

[1] Cawelti, Gordon, ed. *Handbook of Research on Improving Student Achievement*. 3rd ed. Educational Research Service, 2004.

Critical Information Skills for the Re-Create Model

Use Primary Sources
Students will collect and analyze primary sources of information.

When students analyze photographs or artifacts from a time period, they are working with primary information. Historical primary sources can make the past come alive for students. To optimize these resources, students need to learn how to interpret and analyze them. Technology has made it possible to bring many primary artifacts into the classroom virtually.

Read Pictures
Students will decode information from video, pictures in books, and photographs in newspapers and magazines, to discover implicit and explicit information messages they contain.

Illustrations and photographs in both fiction and non-fiction texts hold a wealth of information. While some information is very obvious, much of the information must be uncovered. Students need experiences decoding this kind of visual information, as well as opportunities to analyze it. This skill will prepare students for broader visual literacy skills. These skills are critical to information processing today since so much of the information students access is loaded with powerful images.

Make Connections
Students will work with information to make connections.

There are many "connection building" strategies we can teach to help students understand content. When we suggest that students make connections, we want them to make links to what they already know: what they know about the topic, what they know about reading (viewing/listening) strategies, what they know about webbing/mapping, and how this new content fits into their personal experiences.

Interpret, Infer, Predict
Students will interpret information to develop inferences and make predictions.

Analysis of data in the research process requires that students can take information they have gathered about their topic, examine it closely, and develop personal understanding. They accomplish this by mentally and physically processing the gathered data. Students need to interpret the meaning of the texts they are reading, viewing or listening to; make some inferences about the data based on text clues and prior knowledge and experiences; then apply their interpretation and inferences to making a personal prediction.

Respond to Text
Students will analyze an information text by reacting to the data on a personal level.

As students read, view, and listen to the information, they need to learn how to process information by responding to it and interacting with it. Help students to make connections between what they see, hear, or read and what they already know. Provide students with a variety of strategies so that eventually they will be able to self-select the strategies that are most effective for the information they are working with.

Impact
Students will analyze information to determine impact.

Determining impact is a complex multifaceted skill. Students must be able to first determine effects of an event and then make sure they have examined all relevant perspectives. They must be able to analyze for positive and negative spin-offs of the event. Finally students have to weigh all of this analysis, make links with other knowledge they have, and then evaluate the overall impact.

Examples of the Re-Create Model

Unit 39: Back to the Future   Gr. 7–10

How can digging into past history help us today and tomorrow?

Select

Assemble a collection of excellent time-travel novels at appropriate reading levels and interests. Select novels that travel back in time. Introduce the novels and the guiding question. Students select a novel of interest and try it out. If after the first few pages they are not hooked, ask them to try another one until they find the just right book for this project.

Explore

Students read their novels independently. Provide them with sticky notes and ask them to keep track of interesting place names, historical events, dates, and people encountered when the protagonist travels back in time. Arrange meeting times so students can have discussions about the books they are reading and the places and events encountered in the time travel.

Research

When the novel is finished, ask students to create an event line from the data they collected while reading the novel. Arrange for students to have ample time and guidance researching the time period and location their novel travels back to.

Construct

Show students examples of Jackdaws containing primary artifacts about a period of time. Instruct students to create a jackdaw about the time travel in the novel they just read. They can include maps, letters, diaries, photos, sketches music, art, and artifacts all related to the story. The jackdaws can be physical or electronic collections.

Perform

Invite another class(es) to meet with students so they can present their novels through the jackdaws. If the jackdaws are electronic, they can be mounted on the school library web page for all to discover. Ask students to discuss the guiding question after presentations.

So What?

Arrange for a visit by an author who writes time travel or historical fiction to discuss the importance of research in preparing to write.

Unit 40: Model Parents   Gr. 9–12

What are the attributes of good parents?

Select

This model is excellent for planning the culmination of a unit on parenting in a family studies class. With a partner, students will write and perform a docudrama demonstrating good parenting.

Explore

Introduce this topic with a carefully selected video that demonstrates both positive and negative parenting. As a class, debrief the video and develop a "That's Good, That's Bad" chart from their discussion. Ask students for more examples to expand the chart beyond the video content.

Research

Pair students. Pairs target an age group and research characteristics of children and strategies for supporting the healthy development of this group. Remind students that validation of sources is a critical for this assignment. They should look at the whole child in terms of development: nutrition, safety, mental health, physical health, discipline, learning support, and enrichment.

Construct

Students need to develop a plan for their skit and consult with a teacher before proceeding with actual writing of the script. Once the script is drafted, arrange for peer consultations and build in revision and practicing time.

Perform

Ensure that students have a comfortable space for presenting their docudramas. Videotape the performances so students can critique and set goals for improvement.

So What?

The videoed docudramas can be used for follow-up, problem-solving exercises.

Unit 41: Quotation Marks   Gr. 7–12

Why are these quotations so important? What purpose do they serve?

Select
This strategy will work well with any discipline when you want to highlight some major contributors to a specialty area or explore the major players during an event or era. Select the quotations that will lead students to important concepts and knowledge.

Explore
Write the selected quotations at the top of sheets of chart paper and mount them all around the classroom. Have students do a gallery walk and read all the quotations, pausing to add comments and questions when they want to respond. Ensure students have enough time to read all the quotes and think about them. Ask students to select one of the quotes that is of interest them to use in this project.

Research
Individually, students conduct research about the quote and the life and contributions of the person quoted. They need to research the context of the quote, the time and event or work that it came from, as well as the reasons for its endurance.

Construct/Perform
Students will plan to deliver the quote to the class, in role, taking care to create an accurate atmosphere. Continuing in the role of the quoted person, the student will explain when and why his/her words will remain important in the future.

Big Picture
Provide students with an organizer of all the quotes and space for them to jot down key ideas as they re-create and perform their moments in history. Have students meet in groups to discuss the guiding questions and any other emerging concepts they have discovered regarding the event, era, or discipline framing this project. Share group ideas with the entire class.

Quotes about Quotations

"Stay at home in your mind. Don't recite other people's opinions. I hate quotations. Tell me what you know."

-Ralph Waldo Emerson 1803-1882, American Poet, Essayist

"I often quote myself. It adds spice to my conversation."

- George Bernard Shaw 1856-1950, Irish-born British Dramatist

"It is a good thing for an uneducated man to read a book of quotations."

-Winston Churchill 1874-1965, British Statesman, Prime Minister

Unit 42: Step In-Step About-Step Out   Gr. 6–8

What was life like for working children in the late 19th and early 20th century?

Select
One hundred and fifty years ago, only the children of the wealthy were educated. Most other children worked at home, in the fields, in mines, and even in factories at a very young age. Collect archival photographs of children at work in various jobs. You could print, reference, and mount them like an old album, or select from archival Internet sites and bookmark them.

Explore
Explore a video about working children to introduce the topic (e.g. *Pit Pony* Produced by Cochran Entertainment or *Chandler's Mill* produced by the National Film Board of Canada). Introduce the guiding question and display the photos. Display *Picture Prompts* to guide their picture reading. Allow all students time to view all the photos and then select a photo they are very curious about.

Research
Invite students to step into the picture and project themselves back in time until they are right there with the child. Ask students to step about inside the photo. What do they see, hear, and smell? Have students use *Step In-Step About-Step Out* to record their findings and then develop lots of questions they want to ask the child in the photo. Have students research in the library to discover as much as possible about the time period, work, and life of children.

Construct
Now ask students to step out of the photo and use their research notes and the photo to reconstruct a day or a series of days in the child's life in the form of diary entries.

Perform
Students create a museum type exhibit with the photo, diary entries, and perhaps an artifact such as a piece of clothing, button, ribbon, or coin.

So What?
Share all the experiences in and out of the photo and begin conversations about child labor laws, UN rights of the child, and child labor today. A great book to build discussion around is *If you could wear my sneakers,* by Sheree Fitch. Toronto: Doubleday Canada.1997. (A unique collection of funny poems addressing some of the rights of the child as the UN Convention on the Rights of the Child.)

Gathering Evidence of Understanding
- meaningful information was gleaned from photos
- question storming was productive and relevant
- data selected was useful and accurate
- exhibits showed understanding of the era, child's role, and the impact of child labor on the lives of these children

InfoSkills
- use primary sources
- read pictures
- make connections
- interpret, infer
- respond to text
- impact

Reflect, Rethink, Redesign
- Who could help me find old photos?
  - heritage groups
  - historical boards
  - seniors groups
  - local archives
  - nonfiction books
  - Internet archives
  - specialized libraries
  - newspaper archives
- How did students react to the experiences of child laborers? Why?
- Were they able to connect information and respond in role? What could I do to help those having difficulty?
- Do students make connections between the experiences of these children and current child labor laws?

Note
This lesson idea was inspired by a task in *What do I do about the kid who? 50 ways to turn teaching into learning,* by Kathy Lundy, Pembroke Publishers.

Step In - Step About - Step Out

Step in to the photograph/picture you have selected. **Step about** and observe your surroundings.

What do you see?	What do you hear?	What do you smell?

Make lists of all the questions you have now about the place you are in.

Step out of the photograph or picture now. How can you find the answers to all your questions? Who can help? Make a plan.

Picture Prompts

Where is this scene located?

What is happening in the picture?

What might have happened just prior to the picture?

What might happen next?

Who do you see in the picture?

Who do you not see that might be involved? Why?

What might happen after the picture?

Reinventing a Better Way Model

Reinventing a Better Way Model
(Systems Analysis)

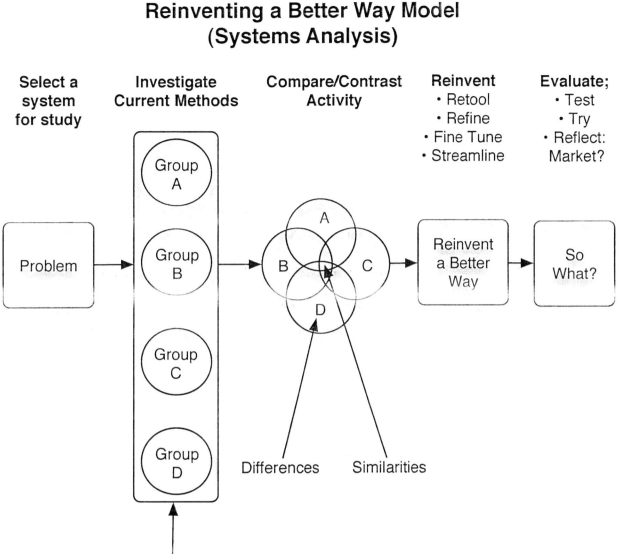

Select a system for study | **Investigate Current Methods** | **Compare/Contrast Activity** | **Reinvent** • Retool • Refine • Fine Tune • Streamline | **Evaluate;** • Test • Try • Reflect: Market?

Problem

Group A

Group B

Group C

Group D

A

B   C

D

Differences   Similarities

Reinvent a Better Way

So What?

Critical Information Point

Why Use This Model?

• Much of our economy depends on efficiency
• Prepares for competitions (best ideas)
• Production and marketing plans and Patents
• Stimulates creativity
• Simulates authentic problems
• Builds group work skills
• Saves time, money, natural resources, and energy

Possible Topics:

• New ways to handle school problems
• Living within a family's means
• Ways to save money, time, and effort
• Create a labor-saving device
• Solving a pesky real-life problem

Critical Information Literacy Skills*

• Use Primary Sources. K&Z p. 46
• Make Connections, K&Z p. 116
• Use Organizers, K&Z p. 90
• Synthesize, K&Z p. 146
• Reflect, Transfer & Apply, K&Z p. 165

* Koechlin, Carol and Sandi Zwaan. *Build Your Own Information Literate School.* Hi Willow, 2003.

Notes on the Reinventing a Better Way Model
(Systems Analysis)

Reinvention usually consists of encountering a problem, examining various ways of solving that problem, and then creating a new, more efficient way to solve the problem.

Examples from everyday life:
- A battery-powered toothbrush
- A hybrid automobile (combining a gasoline engine and a battery-powered engine)
- A new design for an overpass that eliminates congestion.

Examples from school:
- A new way to check in and out textbooks to cut the time spent.
- Discovering new ways to handle discipline problems in the classroom (student-driven study and conclusion)
- Creating a system of a rotating a classroom collection from the library so that there is always something interesting at hand to read.

Problems from curricular areas:
- Four families are trying to survive on $900 a month. None are doing very well. Can we provide suggestions?
- The goal of a physical education class is to maximize the amount of physical exercise in a given period of time (heart rate elevated to a certain rate for a given period of time). What is the best way? What would be the most fun for participants?
- Four different states are trying new health care plans and our state wants to adopt the best one that costs the least. What do we suggest?
- The swamp out in back of the school stinks and neighbors want it paved over. Can we suggest any alternatives to an asphalt acre?
- The pioneers/US government tried to teach Native Americans farming methods since migration for food was becoming more impossible. Why did this effort often fail? (Efficiency might work, but does it make things better?)

In this model, students will encounter a problem that invites an analysis of a system. They are separated into groups to study various methods of solving the problem, then come together to compare and contrast their findings. At this point, creativity supposedly kicks in to challenge them to reinvent a better way. Problems can be created from:
- The way a student acts or performs
- Happenings or procedures in the classroom
- School-wide issues
- Curricular studies in most disciplines
- State standards where compare/contrast is a core activity

Students are challenged to create a new system that will:
- Be more efficient
- Save time and/or money
- Make an impact on larger systems (such as the environment)
- Be less work, easier to do, or more interesting
- Solve the problem at hand and other problems at the same time
- Be more culturally sensitive
- Actually solve a problem rather than create others

Students may discover that a new way is not necessarily superior to the old way of doing things; they may realize that change for change's sake is not productive. However, when students discover systems that don't work well, they might propose work-arounds, alternatives, and loopholes to accomplish a task.

One of the reasons this model has been called "reinvent" rather than "invent" is that true invention, or "thinking outside the box," may take place in an environment other than a resource-abundant setting. True invention often ignores much of the knowledge that is currently known or summarized from a field or discipline. For example, the doctor who discovered that stomach ulcers were caused by a bacteria, rather than an overproduction of acid, was laughed off the podium when he first presented his paper. He discounted the previous research in his quest to build a new hypothesis and a new solution to the problem. Wise teachers recognize in students truly inventive or novel ideas and encourage the thinking of a possibly budding Einstein or Edison.

Technology

One of the most common ways to reinvent a system is to use flowcharting software such as Omnigraffle to chart the old system and diagram its replacement. The investigation of current systems might also require technologies such as email and teleconferencing to consult various experts.

The illustrations in many books will often help students visualize how things work, how the pyramids were built, how underground utility systems are laid out, how medieval castles were constructed, and many other exciting two-dimensional representations of systems. A number of computer modeling systems also allow students to construct a system and enter that system in a three-dimensional simulation. Special add-on visual tools such as video cards will allow 3D modeling and animation. Such tools will be extremely motivating to students as they experience new ways of representing their ideas.

Critical Information Skills for the Reinvent Model

Use Primary Sources
Students will collect and analyze primary sources of information.

Sometimes the best source of information for a research topic is a primary source. When students are required to conduct an interview or a survey, they are gathering original primary data. When students analyze photographs or artifacts from a time period, they are also working with first hand information. Primary sources have the potential to be very engaging for students because they are real, not second hand. Historical primary sources can make the past come alive for students. To optimize these resources, students need to learn how to interpret and analyze them. Technology has made it possible to bring many primary artifacts into the classroom virtually.

Make Connections
Students will work with information to make connections.

There are many "connection building" strategies we can teach to help students understand content. When we suggest that students make connections, we want them to make links to what they already know, what they know about the topic, what they know about reading (viewing/listening) strategies, what they know about webbing/mapping, and how this new content fits into their personal experiences.

Use Organizers
Students will use graphic organizers to help analyze and synthesize data.

Graphic organizers are very useful processing tools. Like any other tools, students need to be taught how to use them. Then they need to be given the support to adapt, modify, and ultimately create their own.

Synthesize
Students will synthesize information to answer their inquiry question and/or create something new.

Only after careful analysis can students begin productive synthesis. When they synthesize, students take the parts identified and put them back together again in a new, more meaningful way. Through synthesis students build understanding and create new personal knowledge.

Reflect, Transfer and Apply
Students will reflect on their work, and transfer and apply their learning to new situations.

This stage of the research process marks the end of the immediate information task and sets the stage for further investigations or applications of the new learning. Students must have metacognitive experiences all through the process as well as at the completion of their sharing, in order for real learning to occur. Always provide students with clear indicators of success such as rubrics and checklists before research begins.

Examples of the Reinvent Model
Unit 43: Bully Help   Gr. 2–4

How can we help each other to solve conflicts and problems?

Investigate Current Methods

Read *The Grouchy Ladybug* by Eric Carl. Discuss feelings in the story. List words that describe feelings. Discuss the term "bully". Ask: "Have you ever been bullied? How did you feel? How do you think the bully felt? Why do you think people bully?" Group students and give them books, at their reading level, that deal with bullying. These picture books will match several reading levels and interests. There are many more that will work for this theme.

Group1 *Willy the Champ* by Anthony Brown
Group 2 *Goggles* by Ezra Jack Keats
Group 3 *Bootsie Barker Bites* by Barbara Bottner and Peggy Rothman
Group 4 *Arthur's April Fool* by Marc Brown
Group 5 *Berenstein Bears and the Bully* by Stan and Jan Berenstein
Group 6 *Taking Care of Crumley* by Ted Staunton

Students read the story in their groups then take turns reading the story aloud again and stopping to fill in the columns on the organizer *Bully Help*. Everyone has a copy to take to the study group.

Compare /Contrast

Form new study groups with one student from each reading group. Ask students to share charts and examine all the different kinds of resolutions. Groups share different resolutions of conflicts.

Reinvent

Ask students to now talk about other ways of solving problems, dealing with frustrations, and dealing with bullies. Ask each group to make up a bully story that illustrates how we can all work toward resolving conflicts. How can we help both the victim and the bully? Give students puppets or have them make sock, finger or bag puppets so they can dramatize their bully story.

Evaluate

Have each group perform their drama, ask, and respond to questions from the other groups.

So What?

Have the groups travel to other classrooms and present their bully plays.

Unit 44: Too Long   Gr. 5–8

For many of the students who ride the bus to and from school, the ride seems way too long. *How can we still pick up all students and drop them off but do it in less time?*

Investigation

Select a manageable number of routes that impact students in the class. Create bus route groups and give them maps of the school area. Each group must discover how the current system works and why. Instruct groups to survey student riders to discover where and at what time they are picked up and dropped off. Groups need to document addresses of pickup and drop off points and numbers of students picked up and or dropped off at each stop then develop maps of current bus routes. Groups should interview experts (bus drivers, school administrators, police officers and parents) to obtain all the data regarding traffic, safety, and special needs.

Compare/Contrast

Have each group mark the route, number of pickups and drop-offs per stop on a large bulletin board map. Using different colored string or yarn for each route so they can see the overall picture. Groups compare maps looking for things such as streets covered, times, and overlap.

Reinvent

Groups will use their own data and look at the overall picture and try to identify ways to reorganize or combine the routes or pickup points to make the rides take up less time. Reconvene as a class. Share ideas for improvement and select the ideas most likely to work.

So What?

Prepare a class report to share suggestions with a representative from the school district. Sometimes looking at a situation from a different perspective can help find a new and more efficient way to do it. Have students brainstorm other situations they might be able to "reinvent" to improve.

Unit 45: Faster, Higher, Stronger   Gr. 9–12

How can we improve the Olympics so the games truly reflect all athletes' accomplishments?

Problem

Introduce the Olympic motto "Citius, Altius, Fortius": Faster Higher, Stronger. Pair students to discuss its meaning. Share as a class and discuss. Pair again to share all the positives about the Olympic Games, the negatives, and the questionable. Share with the class, cluster ideas, and develop a list of major problems to overcome (e.g. doping, judging, cheating, advertising, politics, financial support to athletes, security, media coverage, stress and bias etc.). Collectively decide how many of the issues the class wants to deal with and develop focus groups to study them.

Investigation

Remind groups to explore all the relevant perspectives and validate and accurately document their sources. Brainstorm possible sources and/or provide URLs of the IOCE, official athletic associations, national support programs, etc. Encourage groups to share data they find that could help another group. The recorder in each group keeps accurate notes of their findings, and provides group members with a copy for sharing in the next stage.

Compare/Contrast

JigSaw students to form study groups. Share findings. Keep track of similarities or differences in the information shared. Look for patterns and trends in the collective data. Students use *Inductive Reasoning* organizer to help them develop substantiated generalizations about their collective findings.

Reinvent

Reconvene in home groups; share relationships and generalizations discovered. Review the guiding question. Home groups should now be able to make a few suggestions about ways the Olympics could be re-invented to address the problem their group focused on. Students use *Reinvent the Olympics* organizer test out their solution ideas, citing the strengths, weakness and considerations of each. Then decide on their best solution ideas. Share and chart the suggestions from each group. Work with the class to develop the top 10 things the Olympic Commission should do to improve the Olympic Games.

So What?

Have the students formally present their top 10 ideas to the committee planning the next Olympic Games as well as to the athletic associations and other major decision makers.

Gathering Evidence of Understanding

- o adequate number and good variety of issues were identified
- o both positive and negative perspectives were included
- o inductive reasoning organizer indicates prompts were used as a guide
- o ideas generated are practical and practicable

InfoSkills

- o use primary sources
- o use organizers
- o make connections
- o synthesize - consider alternative ideas
- o reflect, transfer and apply

Reflect, Rethink, Redesign

- o Are students having difficulty coming up with problems? Could I arrange to have them skim some selected articles that dealt with such issues during previous Olympic Games?
- o Are students familiar with the JigSaw strategy? Are there some who require a review?
- o Did grouping work smoothly? Is there something I can do to make it easier?
- o Do students understand how the reasoning prompts help them as they consider alternatives and decide on best solutions?

Bully Help

Read your story. Think about the characters and the problems they had. Talk about it and then work with your group to complete this organizer.

Title	Bully Who is teasing? Who is being mean? Who is selfish? Who is hurting someone?	Victim Who is being hurt? Who is afraid? Who is crying? Who is running away or hiding?	Resolution What helped the victim? What helped the bully?	Ending How well did the resolution help? Do you have some other ideas to try?
Setting Where does the story happen?				

Inductive Reasoning

Guiding Question:

Examine your data.

Look for patterns, connections and relationships.

What do these links tell you?

How can you explain the relationships you see?

Given the links you have discovered, what is probable?

Make some thoughtful generalizations.

Make some inferences based on your observations.

Organize the data and test out your ideas.

Do you have enough quality data to back up your reasoning?

Be careful. Don't jump to faulty conclusions!

If....

Then...

Reinvent the Olympics

Focus Problem

Solution Ideas	Strengths	Weaknesses	Considerations	Analysis

Based on this analysis, the best possible solutions are:

The Quest Model

The Quest Model
(The Well-Designed Research, Experiment, or Project)

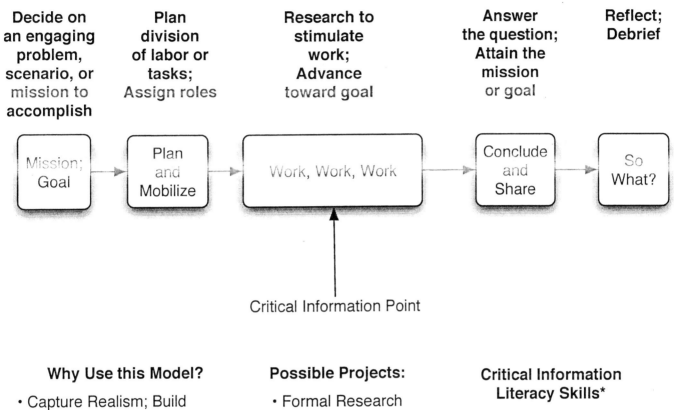

Decide on an engaging problem, scenario, or mission to accomplish	Plan division of labor or tasks; Assign roles	Research to stimulate work; Advance toward goal	Answer the question; Attain the mission or goal	Reflect; Debrief
Mission; Goal	Plan and Mobilize	Work, Work, Work	Conclude and Share	So What?

Critical Information Point

Why Use this Model?

- Capture Realism; Build Expertise
- Build responsibility and independence
- Prepare for college or a profession
- Build a sense of achievement
- Capitalize on natural curiosities
- Make the curriculum relevant
- Develop deep understanding

Possible Projects:

- Formal Research Paper
- Web Quest
- I-Search Paper
- Simulation Game
- Scientific challenge/ competition
- Senior Paper
- Independent Study
- Recital

Critical Information Literacy Skills*

- Define and Clarify, K&Z p. 1
- Locate and Retrieve, K&Z p. 23
- Select, Process, and Record Data, K&Z p. 51
- Analyze, K&Z p. 89
- Synthesize, K&Z p. 145
- Share and Use, K&Z p. 155
- Reflect, Transfer, and Apply, K&Z p. 165
- Adding It All Up, K&Z, p 173

* Koechlin, Carol and Sandi Zwaan. *Build Your Own Information Literate School*. Hi Willow, 2003.

Notes on the Quest Model

The Quest Model encompasses the more traditional forms of library research done in schools plus popular research-based ideas that lend themselves to student research. Examples include:

- Reports
- Research Papers
- Web Quests
- I-Search papers
- Become an Expert

Each presumes the availability of a high-quality information system in both print and digital form. These projects have also become the areas where the most plagiarism occurs.

Recently, ABC News did a special on the rampant plagiarism in the nation's elite colleges and universities. Students often paid to have professionals write their research papers, or they simply downloaded sample papers from the Internet for a hefty fee. Commentators attributed the problem to a lack of morals and dishonesty in the rising generation but said nothing about the ineptitude of teachers who make blanket research assignments that invite such a response. If one says to a group of students, "Write a research paper on a topic of your choice," it is tantamount to authorizing and recommending plagiarism.

Many years ago, when *Cliffs Notes* were first published, the English teachers of this nation arose in indignation because so many of their students were cutting and clipping from this source when critical analysis was assigned. They marched on libraries, asking that such publications be banned. Librarians refused. English teachers finally realized that the problem was not in the existence of *Cliffs Notes,* it was in the nature of the assignments. Today, a common technique in the English classroom is to create an assignment in such a way that students cannot cut and clip a final product; rather, they can use the cut and clip to create a unique product not available in any information system. It's known as the "clever assignment."

Another common technique teachers use is to prescribe the types and quantities of information resources that are allowable in some sort of research assignment. An example would be, "Write a three-page paper; don't use an encyclopedia; cite three magazine articles, two books, and one Internet site." Librarians generally oppose such structure simply because this regiment of resources might not exist for a particular topic a student might choose. A superior strategy for the teacher is to require the defense of every information source cited in the assignment. Using this method, the student will be accustomed not only to finding resources, but also to sorting and sifting carefully.

In the pages that follow, some guidance for dealing with various types of the Quest Model is given. All of these compare traditional ways of assigning tasks in an information-poor environment vs. an information-rich one.

Technology

For more formal research, writing tools such as word processors, computerized thesauri, automated dictionaries, and spelling checkers are essential components. If the research goes beyond a written product, then tools for the creation of audio, video, or Internet sites will require requisite software.

Technology is essential in the research process as students search for information sources, take notes, and compose citations. Information spaces such as Questia.com provide an online library and a paper-creation workspace. Within this workspace, quotations or notes can be clipped as electronic books are read on screen. Additionally, software will automatically bring the citation, with any notations, onto the workspace. Thus, the teacher reading such a paper online sees not only the student's work, but also the full text and citations from which the ideas came.

In another program titled Power Researcher, students can capture web pages, PDF documents, and organize them as you would a set of notes. This management system can be viewed over time by a teacher who is monitoring a student's activities. Again, the final product can contain original sources, citations, and extracts easily accessed by the reader.

These are but two examples of innovative products beyond the concept of a simple word processor. The writing process becomes as interesting and as manageable as the final product in an instructor's assessment of learning.

The Common Report: A Few Cautions

Teachers often want students to extend their surface knowledge and get some experience doing library research at the same time. Such exploration is a healthy ideal since surface knowledge of a topic is rarely enough to claim any kind of a quality education.

For the library, the librarian and/or technology specialist, one form of this common assignment is to be avoided like the plague.

If the teacher says: "Do a three-page report on a topic of your choice," the likely result is a plagiarized report—particularly when the Internet is easily available.

Equally frustrating to libraries are the rules issued by many teachers governing the report:

> Do a three-page report on a topic of your choice.
> - You may not use an encyclopedia.
> - You may use two periodical articles and one book
> - You may not use the Internet

Such rules, while well intentioned, put requirements on the information system that may be impossible to follow. There may not be two periodical articles on the topic in question; the Internet may be the best source for this topic; the encyclopedia may be the best place for a clueless student to begin.

What are better rules that work in any library or digital information system?

- Use a variety of information sources for your report (print, digital, and the Internet).
- You must defend each of the sources you use as the highest quality available (the most authoritative, the most current, the most believable, and from the most reliable sources/publishers/experts, etc.)

Computer programs, such as Power Researcher, provide students with a workspace along side of a word processor. These workspaces allow students to capture pieces of the original sources they use and drag them along with their citations on to their desktop work area. Students create their report or research paper using these original resources, and the final product contains both the student product and the original sources they used. For teachers who eliminate paper and have all students submit reports or research electronically, such tools are incredibly useful in assessing what a student knows and the path they took to create their product. We predict that many such tools will soon be available to teachers and students everywhere.

The Research Paper: Models for Student Use

Many librarians currently teach some sort of research model that lays out the steps of the research process for the students. In some schools, a research model is adopted for the entire school so that students have an opportunity to become proficient in it, whether doing papers for social studies, science, or the language arts. There are a number of popular research models being used in North America. Ask a school librarian for their personal choice. For elementary school, librarians often simplify the model into fewer steps, but the concept of following a model based on the scientific method of research is common.

The generic model below shows steps in the model; the model is circular indicating that students often skip around the model as they work, rather than doing their project sequentially.

The Information Literacy Process

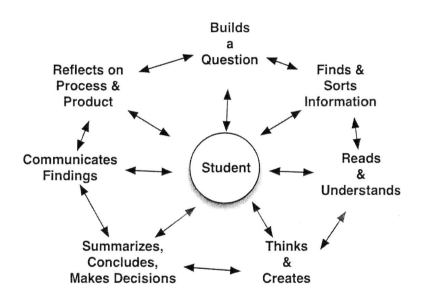

On the following two pages, a variation of the above research model is presented in the left column, with micro research skills being elaborated in the center column, and comments about how these skills flourish in an information-rich and technology-rich environment in the left column.

Readers who remember scrounging magazine articles from library magazine rooms after copying many citations from the *Reader's Guide* will appreciate how times have changed.

Research Process Model

Stages of Research: Macro-skills	Description of Stages: Micro-Skills	Supported by an Information Rich and Technology Rich Environment
Define and Clarify	• Understand the research process • Explore a topic • Define a research topic • Develop questions • Develop keywords • Develop a plan	• Access to excellent resources to support all curriculum topics at all levels. • Variety of resource types (e.g. print, electronic, video, primary sources, speakers, and field trips) • Access to resources 24x7 from school and from home • Instruction in effective questioning skills • Instruction in understanding and planning a research task. • Time management, organization tools and models • Consultation and learning advice
Locate and Retrieve	• Use search strategies • Locate resources • Skim, scan, and consider • Evaluate resources • Design surveys • Use primary sources	• Instruction in effective search strategies, and retrieval skills • Tools and support to evaluate and validate resources • Instruction in the location and use of primary sources
Select Process and Record	• Pre-reading strategies • Actively read, view, and listen • Select relevant data • Determine fact • Read pictures • Use features of non-fiction text • Note-making • Legal and ethical use of information and ideas	• Instruction in note taking, summarizing, and critical analysis of data. • Information experts • Organizers and referencing tools • On-line support
Analyze	• Use organizers • Sort • Compare • Classify • Identify and investigate patterns and trends • Respond to text • Make connections • Cause and effect	• Organizers and software available to assist with analysis and interpretation of data • Modeling of analysis techniques • Consultation with information experts

	• Impact • Interpret, infer, and predict • Understand perspective • Collaborate	
Synthesize	• Develop generalizations and report. • Consider alternatives and make a judgment or prediction. • Draw conclusions. • Make decisions. • Gain perspective and develop an argument or a thesis. • Explore solutions and solve a problem or construct a new hypothesis.	• Consultation with information experts and learning advice • Organizers and modeling of synthesis techniques
Share and Use	• Decide on the best format. • Develop a plan. • Utilize appropriate technologies. • Cite all information sources. • Test ideas and practice. • Communicate new learning.	• Sophisticated communications hardware and software • Instruction in designing and presenting • Exemplars of good products
Reflect, Transfer and Apply	• Reflect on the process and the product • Self-evaluate effort and accomplishments • Set goals for both short term and long term improvement • Apply new learning to other experiences and disciplines • Take informed action based on research, discoveries, and conclusions	• Tools to assist with assessment and goal setting • School-wide, cross-curricular information skills integration

Based on Koechlin and Zwaan, *Build Your Own Information Literate School*

The I-Search Paper

High school English teachers have widely adopted the I-Search research process as the structure for teaching the traditional research report or paper. Based on Ken Macrorie's 1988 book entitled *The I-Search Paper*, numerous adaptations have been made. One such version is the one done by *Make It Happen!* at http://www2.edc.org/FSC/ MIH/index.html, and numerous printed guides have been published.

The basic steps of I-Search change slightly depending on who is describing the process. Here is one of the variants in five steps:
1. My question
2. My search process
3. What I have learned
4. What this means to me
5. References

Doing an I-Search paper in an information-rich environment would seem to be both sensible and necessary. However, many teachers try to implement the model even when resources and information is substandard. As one can readily guess, the products of such efforts are likely to be substandard as well.

On the following page, we outline the five-step process, and add detail in the center column of the table about the research process. We then provide some essential tips for conducting such a project in an information-rich environment.

I-Search

Instructional Phases	Description of Phase	Supported by an Information Rich and Technology Rich Environment
My Question	• Immersion in theme • Posing the I-Search question	• Access to excellent resources to support all curriculum topics at all levels • Variety of resource types (e.g. print, electronic, video, primary sources, speakers, field trips) • Access to resources • 24/7 from school and from home • Instruction in effective search strategies, and questioning skills
My Search Process	• Designing a search plan	• Instruction in understanding and planning a research task. • Time management and organization tools and models • Consultation and learning advice
What I Have Learned	• Gathering and summarizing information • Analyzing and synthesizing to construct new knowledge	• Instruction in note taking, summarizing, and critical analysis of data. • Organizers and software available to assist with analysis and interpretation of data • Modeling of analysis techniques • Consultation with information experts
What This Means to Me	• Drafting, editing and publishing the I-Search report or paper or project. • Assessing growth as a researcher	• Sophisticated communications hardware and software • Instruction in designing and presenting • Exemplars of good products • Tools to assist with assessment and goal setting
References		• Information experts • Organizers and referencing tools • On-line support

Based on *Make It Happen!* The I-Search Unit http://www2.edc.org/FSC/MIH/

The WebQuest as a Research Model

The WebQuest, the brainchild of Bernie Dodge, has become a popular way to have students use the Internet as a research tool. The teacher creates an engaging quest, dividing students into various role groups on a mission to solve a problem. Each team then contributes their knowledge to the solution of the quest as a whole.

On the following page, a typical WebQuest is diagramed with suggestions for doing it in an information-rich environment. The main WebQuest web site is also listed to facilitate exploration of the hundreds of examples that are posted there.

Like all good ideas in education, there are hundreds of good and even great WebQuests that have been published. There are also hundreds more that are poor examples both in their conception and their potential for failure with real students.

We have two quarrels with WebQuests:

- When poorly designed, they often do not result in the higher-level thinking that Bernie Dodge intended when he created and promoted the model.

- They use only one information source—the Internet, when the best and most authoritative information on a particular topic may come from print, digital, or multimedia sources.

Our recommendations for doing WebQuests and doing them well in information-rich environments include:

- Formulate the original quest so that students will have to use higher-level thinking skills to solve the problem or achieve the goal.

- Include the requirement that students find and use high quality information sources regardless of the medium.

One could say that the latter requirement transforms the model from a WebQuest to an InfoQuest. Guilty as charged.

Building Blocks of a WebQuest

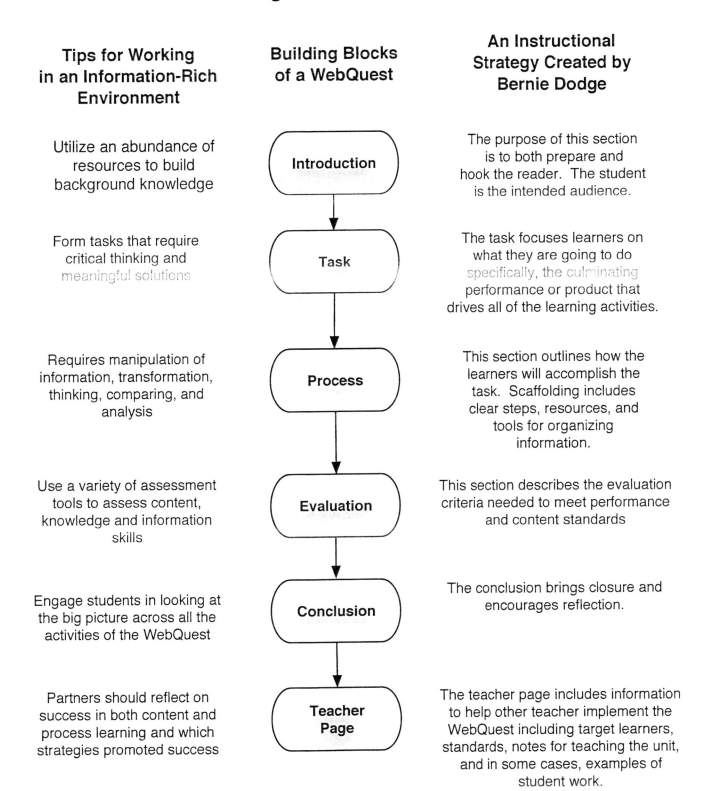

Tips for Working in an Information-Rich Environment

Utilize an abundance of resources to build background knowledge

Form tasks that require critical thinking and meaningful solutions

Requires manipulation of information, transformation, thinking, comparing, and analysis

Use a variety of assessment tools to assess content, knowledge and information skills

Engage students in looking at the big picture across all the activities of the WebQuest

Partners should reflect on success in both content and process learning and which strategies promoted success

Building Blocks of a WebQuest

Introduction

Task

Process

Evaluation

Conclusion

Teacher Page

An Instructional Strategy Created by Bernie Dodge

The purpose of this section is to both prepare and hook the reader. The student is the intended audience.

The task focuses learners on what they are going to do specifically, the culminating performance or product that drives all of the learning activities.

This section outlines how the learners will accomplish the task. Scaffolding includes clear steps, resources, and tools for organizing information.

This section describes the evaluation criteria needed to meet performance and content standards

The conclusion brings closure and encourages reflection.

The teacher page includes information to help other teacher implement the WebQuest including target learners, standards, notes for teaching the unit, and in some cases, examples of student work.

http://projects.edtech.sandi.net/staffdev/tpss99/mywebquest/t-index.htm

Become an Expert

"I've been crazy about frogs since I was a kid. I collected them along with snakes, ants, and other critters, and even joined the Wisconsin Herpetological Society as a charter member—at age 14. Now, as a zoologist-photographer, I get to combine my two great passions. For a guy like me, an assignment to cover Brazil's Atlantic forest was a ticket to Frog Heaven."
~ Mark W. Moffett, "Frog heaven," *National Geographic,* March, 2004, p. 24.

On winning the Academy Award for 2004, Peter Jackson, Director of *The Lord of the Rings* movies said, "Thanks to my parents who gave me an 8mm movie projector at age nine."

Like the experiences above, teachers often encounter young students who want to explore topics in depth. Kid experts in dinosaurs are legendary, and it is not uncommon to find young docents in dinosaur museums who wow visitors with their vast knowledge. Teachers often encounter computer geeks or children who have traveled the world with their parents and thus know a great deal about global cultures, geography, or political systems.

Public education has usually tried to develop a broad knowledge of many disciplines and ideas. This goal, however, need not conflict with the student who wants to develop expertise. Teachers are wise to cultivate such interests along side the need to be educated broadly.

Libraries, museums, and computer information systems are the best friends of students wanting to become experts in the Antarctic, whales, dinosaurs, science fiction, inventions, or a myriad of other topics. The child may want to do every research paper or project in school on the same topic while we expect them to be more broad and develop other interests as well.

Encourage budding experts to:
 ❖ Explore the school library first
 ❖ Explore the public library
 ❖ Navigate the Internet
 ❖ Link to experts in the field
 ❖ Gain access to advanced collections
 ❖ Do experimentation and research
 ❖ Explore vicarious experiences through film and video
 ❖ Question all information in libraries

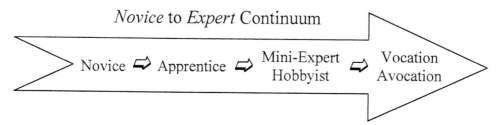

Novice to *Expert* Continuum

Novice ⇨ Apprentice ⇨ Mini-Expert Hobbyist ⇨ Vocation Avocation

Part Three

Dessert:

15. Mix It Up!

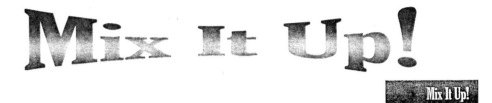

Mix It Up!

(Be Creative in Combining/Modifying All the Models)

Appetizers:

Background to Question Model
Sensemaking Model
Read, View, and Listen Model
Advice to Action Model
Compare and Contrast Model

The Main Course:

The Concept Jigsaw Puzzle Model
The Problems/Possibilities Jigsaw Puzzle Model
The Matrix Model
The Timeline Model
The History and Mystery Model
Take a Position Model
The Re-Create Model
The Reinventing a Better Way Model
The Quest Model

Examples:

• Do a Major Background to Question study before a Quest
• Do a Matrix before having to Take a Position
• Sensemake a problem before trying to Reinvent it
• Compare and Contrast as a History/Mystery Model unfolds
• Begin with a Jigsaw and then culminate with a Matrix

Notes on Mix It Up!

Part of the fun of teaching and the motivation to continue through the years comes from combining lots of good ideas in education into something that works well with the students in our classroom and in our school. As stated in the introduction of this book, the 15 models do not ask teachers to throw out any of the creative and exciting learning experiences they already use. Rather, we envision tweaks in the instructional design that will push higher-level thinking into a position of prominence in the classroom and in the library.

For dessert, use features of the previous 14 models to make sense of a particular learning experience at your grade level or in your topical area. We encourage the use of creativity, spontaneity, and the mixing of the various models over and over until deep understanding develops. If any of the models fail, redesign them until an excellent learning experience appears.

When creative teachers use the models, they can expect some of these signs of success:
- Motivation will increase
- Interest in the content will rise
- Sound work habits will become commonplace
- Group study and communication skills will increase
- Re-teaching will be at a minimum
- Transference from one unit to another—or from one discipline to another—will be commonplace
- Information handling skills will improve
- Healthy skepticism of information will grow
- Independent learners will become the norm rather than the exception
- Learners will begin to exhibit confidence in their ability to tackle any learning task

On the previous page, examples were given for mixing various models into a single learning experience. One might use the Background to Question Model before launching students into a major Problem/Possibilities Jigsaw Puzzle Model. Such an approach would be important if the diversity of learners in the classroom is so great that the absence of background building would jeopardize the main learning experience. For example, the teachers of an elementary school in New Mexico wanted to involve the children in the construction of an authentic Anasazi village. By doing a month-long background study, they were able to introduce that lost culture to the children, get them excited, and allow them to develop the idea that turned into a year-long, life-sized construction of a village. Experts from many parts of the state, the State Library, the State Archives, and stone construction & tools all combined to make this an unforgettable learning experience.

Yet, creative learning experiences that involve higher-level thinking in information-rich environments need not be year-long experiences. They can be a few days, a few weeks, or even a few months. The time period is not as important as the structure of the learning experience that exploits information and technology.

Examples of the Mix It Up Model
Unit 46: Putting the Wheels in Motion   Gr. 4–6

Many children are seriously injured every year in bicycle accidents. What can we do to reduce these injuries?

Background to Question Model

Provide students with printed statistics of local and national bicycle accidents. Instruct students to work with a partner to interpret the statistics. Provide the organizer, *Analyzing Patterns and Trends*. Have partners meet with a larger group of six and share their analysis of the statistics. Ask the large groups to suggest 3–5 areas that need to be investigated to build background information for the class (e.g. construction of bicycles, types and causes of injuries, safety measures and equipment established or available, education of cyclists, training of motorists, municipal laws and bylaws regarding bicycle riding, and school safety programs).

Concept Jigsaw Model

Specialist Team		Sharing Team	
First Question: What are the current facts and issues regarding bicycle safety?	Form teams of researchers according to their interests in the topics suggested by the exploration team. Because most of the needed information will be acquired through direct requests to local establishments and authorities, it will be necessary to teach or review skills for conducting interviews. Instruct students to prepare their interview questions and conference with their teacher. Ask each investigative team to appoint a moderator and tasks for each team member. Each student will keep a running log of their investigations and the data collected. Each team will keep a portfolio of the collective raw data on their focus topic. Ask each team to summarize their findings and to make copies to take to their study groups.	Concept forming question: What are the causes and effects of bicycle injuries?	Instruct the study teams to share their findings, make connections, and ask questions until they have built a comprehensive picture of the issues surrounding bicycle safety. Have each team develop a web illustrating the complexities of the problem.
Team A School		Team ABCDE	
Team B Municipal		Team ABCDE	
Team C Medical		Team ABCDE	
Team D Police		Team ABCDE	
Team E Industry		Team ABCDE	

Reinvent

Review the guiding question. *What can we do to reduce bicycle injuries to children?*
Based on the work accomplished to date, ask the teams to start to construct some solution ideas. Provide students with the organizer *Problems, Problems* to help them analyze their solution ideas. Share all the group solutions and cluster and reword as necessary. Decide as a class on the top ten recommendations. Develop a flow chart to illustrate possible implementations of these recommendations. Invite available experts to serve as consultants for the class. Arrange for each study group to consult with one of the experts in person (e.g. Doctor/surgeon, Police Officer, city planner, parent, competitive cyclist, or physical education teacher). After the consultation, make any necessary refinements or changes to the recommendations.

So What?

Have students formally present their recommendations to the appropriate decision makers and initiate any recommendations that they can develop independently, such as school safety campaigns.

Unit 47: Packaged Problems   Gr. 4–8

How can changes be made to the way goods are packaged to reduce the amount of garbage?

Compare Contrast Model

The packages currently used for many of the goods householders buy contribute greatly to recycling and garbage that must be collected. This results in storage problems and expensive collection and processing, not to mention the effect on landfill sites.

Instruct groups to brainstorm for different materials used in packaging; share and create a list. Provide students with data (from information pamphlets and /or an invited expert) about materials that are recyclable in your district and procedures for collection of garbage and recyclable materials. Now have students classify the packaging materials as to materials that are recyclable and those that are garbage. Examine a few items that have multiple packaging materials and establish criteria (e.g. garbage, recyclable, partially recyclable or reusable).

Students survey items purchased for their homes and collect packages and packaging materials for a two-week period. They use copies of the *Packages, Packages* chart to keep an ongoing list of items, a description of the packaging and to identify whether it is garbage, recyclable, partially recyclable or reusable.

At the end of the collection period, students use a highlighter to identify those items with packages that are not totally recyclable and then circle the three they feel are most in need of improvement. Students bring to class their completed charts as well as the packages they identified as the worst offenders. Make a class list of problem packages. Sort and cluster like products. Brainstorm questions about how things are packaged and why.

Reinvent

Select a manageable number of problem packages from the class list for further study; group students with like interests. Students use information from their charts to investigate similar packages and packaging materials from different manufacturers. Examine problem packages and identify materials used. Determine whether they are cosmetic or have a specific purpose (e.g. necessary for hygiene, breakage/damage protection, convenience for stacking or shipping, theft and deterrents). Think about what is necessary for shipping, storage, customer safety and display. Consider the materials that are available. Consult manufacturers and store managers. Ask lots of questions: "What other more environmentally friendly materials could do the same job? How could the package be redesigned? Is there another way to display it without the package or with less packaging...?"

Jigsaw students to meet with other groups and examine different packaging problems. Share findings and discuss similarities and differences. Return to home groups and begin the process of designing a more environmentally friendly-package. Create an illustration with a description of materials used or make a prototype of your package.

So What?

Display original packages along with the new and improved packages in a classroom marketplace. Have students describe their packaging and explain its benefits to other students and/or classes. Allow others to ask questions of their fellow packaging engineers.

Unit 48: Grad Trip   Gr. 6–8

Where should the class plan to go for their year-end excursion?

Advice to Action

The graduating class is planning a year-end excursion. They want to consider everyone's preferences, but there are so many other things they need to consider. Ask students to brainstorm with a partner and make some predictions about all the possible considerations (e.g. cost per student, sponsorship, fundraising, and possible locations as well as district regulations regarding chaperones, transportation, accommodation, meals, etc.). Share with the class and develop a list of information needs. Discuss who are the best experts to consult for these concerns. Divide up the tasks and have students gather the needed information.
- Survey students and develop a list of trip preferences.
- Consult parent association
- Consult school administration
- Consult possible sponsors

Hold a class conference to present findings and to decide on the parameters to be set (e.g. cost per student, distance, special needs and accommodations, etc.). Review the preferences of students and the suggested locations of administration and parents. Evaluate the suggested locations based on some of the established parameters and decide on 6–10 possible sites for further investigation.

The Matrix Model

Build a giant matrix on a class bulletin board. Assign a location for each group investigation. As students gather data, pictures, maps, and brochures, they mount them on the class matrix.

Excursion suggestion	Location: Distance, possible travel time, and costs	Accommodation: Possible locations, amenities and costs and availability	Site-seeing: tours and costs	Food choice and costs	Clothing requirements		
1)							
2)							
3)							
4)							
5)							
6)							

Groups analyze their gathered data, and decide on the top three choices. Consult with other groups and select the location preferred by most groups.

So What?

After their excursion, students compile a list of guidelines to assist the next graduating class as they select their year-end excursion.

Unit 49: Time for Technology   Gr. 7–10

How have developments in technology changed our world in the last century?

Background to Question Model

Assign students to work in five groups. Each group will become experts in an area of technological development. Provide each group with an artifact representative of a technological development in their assigned category.

- Health - hearing aid
- Communication - cell phone
- Transportation - electronic plane ticket
- Recreation - ghetto blaster
- Work - computer mouse

Have students generate questions about their artifact. Share and discuss questions looking for patterns (e.g. When was it invented, who invented it, how does it help, what materials is it made from, is it environmentally friendly, what other inventions or developments are similar? etc.).

Timeline Model

Present the engaging question. Have students conduct searches to discover the major technological developments that have occurred in their assigned category: health, communication, transportation recreation and work. Explain that they are looking for the effect and impact technology has had on both humans and the natural environment. Note that they may discover both positive and negative effects. Encourage students to examine the effects of each development from all relevant perspectives. Provide students with the organizer *Tracking Technology Over Time*. Review effective search strategies and best sources for the needed data. When data gathering time is up, have each group cut up their organizer into strips and place the technological developments they have discovered on a large classroom timeline using a different color for each group. See *Tips for Terrific Timelines p. 122*

Give students time to examine the completed timeline and look for patterns, ripple effects, and links. Give students colored string so they can physically make links between developments on the timeline. Follow strings; compare developments to those on other strings. Share findings. Provide each group with a *That's Good That's Bad* (p. 62) organizer. Instruct students to use their original data and the visual timeline to help them analyze the effects of their category in both positive and negative terms.

So What?

Discuss the effects of technological development on both humans and the natural environment. Have each student write a reflective log of the learning experience and set three goals reflecting their hopes for future technological developments.

Unit 50: The Power Struggle   Gr. 9–12

How do power struggles in texts engage the reader?

The Read, View, Listen Model

Students will be reading short stories to explore issues of power, how they are developed through narrative, and what impact they have on the reader. Brainstorm with students the kinds of questions they need to ask themselves as they are reading, if they are to uncover the power scenarios in their text.

Who is in control? How do you know?
How do the powerful characters act? How do the powerless characters act?
Whose voice is clearest? Whose voice is not heard?
Is there a hierarchy of power?
Who is mistreated?

Form small groups and provide each reader with a different short story that demonstrates the theme of power struggles. Students read the text and, using sticky notes, identify evidence of power, powerlessness, and the language that describes power.

Compare and Contrast Model

Instruct students to meet in groups to share the power struggles they have discovered in their short stories. Share also the power language they discovered and the characteristics of positions of power and powerlessness.

Sensemaking Model

Once students have analyzed the relationships in their short stories and compared them to those of their peers, they are ready to demonstrate their understanding. Have students create a concept map of their short story that shows visually the power struggles they discovered. Instruct students to experiment with space, medium, colors, shapes, fonts, and graphics to create the most effective re-conceptualization of their story. Share ideas with their peers; critique each other's work; and prepare a final concept map.

So What?

Share maps and return to the guiding question. Discuss the impact power struggles in narrative have on the reader and the larger community.

Analyzing Patterns and Trends

Look over the data you have gathered. Can you find any patterns or repeated information?

Record any patterns or trends you discover.

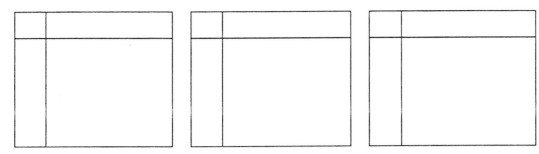

What are the possible reasons for the patterns and trends you have discovered?

- .....
- .....
- .....
- .....

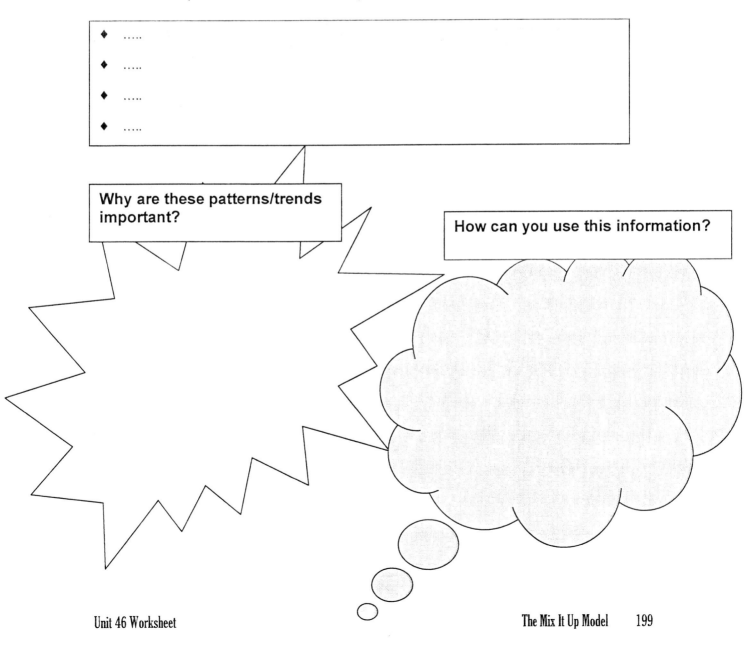

Why are these patterns/trends important?

How can you use this information?

Problems, Problems

Many children are injured every year in bicycle accidents.

What can we do to reduce these injuries?

Causes	Effects

Solution Ideas	Strengths	Weaknesses
1)		
2)		
3)		
4)		
5)		
6)		
The best solution idea...		

Packages, Packages

Product	Packaging Material	Garbage, Recycling, Partial Recycling, Reusable

Tracking Technology Over Time

New Development	Date	Positive impact on humans and the natural environment	Negative impact on humans and the natural environment

Resources We Recommend

Apple Computer. Check out the Apple Computer education program initiative that works with many school districts to install and investigate the integration of computers into every day education. Admittedly promoting computers but full of interesting ideas and experimentation. See their website at: http://www.apple.com/education/k12

Cawelti, Gordon, ed. *Handbook of Research on Improving Student Achievement*. 3rd ed. Educational Research Service, 2004. One of the best easy-to-use summaries of educational research that we continue to consult. It is arranged by subject disciplines and assembled by scholars in each field. The summaries are succinct and cover topics instantly. Useful in the classroom.

Collaborative Evaluation led by Local Educators: A Practical, Print- and Web-Based Guide. NEIR.TEC (Northeast and the Islands Regional Technology in Education Consortium), 2004. Since so many of the models in our book require collaboration between the teacher and the librarian plus technology specialist, this guide to collaborative assessment is an invaluable resource.

Cross, Richard W., Theodor Rebarber, and Justin Torres. *Grading the System: The Guide to State Standards, Tests, and Accountability Policies*. The Thomas B Fordham Foundation, 2004. A state by state guide to what's going on in the entire area of standards and testing.

Daniels, Harvey and Steven Zemelman. *Subjects Matter: Every Teacher's Guide to Content-Area Reading*. Heineman, 2004. Hundreds of good ideas for helping readers be more thoughtful, analyze what they are reading, and see the big picture from reading non-fiction.

enGauge: A Framework for Effective Technology Use in Schools. NCREL: North Central Regional Education Laboratory, 2000. A comprehensive model for examining and implementing education in the digital age and for the digital age learner; a description of the digital age organization. http://engauge.ncrel.org

Farrell, Thomas S.C. *Reflective Practice in Action: 80 Reflection Breaks for Busy Teachers*. Corwin Press, 2004. Because reflection is a basic element for both students and teachers in information-rich environments, this book provides tips for reflecting on a regular basis so that it becomes a regular part of the learning process.

Koechlin, Carol and Sandi Zwaan. *Build Your Own Information Literate School*. Hi Willow Research and Publishing, 2003.

Koechlin, Carol and Sandi Zwaan. *Info Tasks for Successful Learning.* Stenhouse Publishers, 2001.

Krashen, Stephen. *The Power of Reading: Insights from the Research.* Libraries Unlimited, 2004. Krashen's extensive review of reading research supports the notion that wide reading is a major boost to academic achievement as it builds comprehension, grammar, vocabularly, spelling, and general knowledge.

Lazear, David. *Higher-Order Thinking the Multiple Intelligence Way.* Zepher Press, 2004. We appreciate David Lazear's clear presentation of Howard Gardner's work and the practical way higher-order thinking is demonstrated in sample units of instruction.

Learning for the 21st Century: A Report and Mile Guide for 21st Century Skills. Partnership for 21st Century Skills, 2003. A major document and rubric of the integration of technology into education sponsored by many organizations. See www.21stcenturyskills.org

Loertscher, David V. and Blanche Woolls. *Information Literacy: A Review of the Research.* 2nd ed. Hi Willow Research & Publishing, 2002. A comprehensive look at the behavior of children and teenagers as they confront information during the research process.

Marzano, Robert J. *Building Background Knowledge for Academic Achievement: Research on What Works in Schools.* ASCD, 2004. The first full-length volume we have seen on this topic, Marzano builds a strong case for spending more time building background knowledge before the main event begins—particularly for children with varying cultural and language backgrounds.

Marzano, Robert J., Debra J. Pickering, and Jane E. Pollock. *Classroom Instruction that Works: Research-Based Strategies for Increasing Student Achievement.* ASCD, 2003. While not comprehensive, this book examines a number of well-researched techniques that schools can use with confidence. School-level factors, teacher-level factors, and student-level factors are examined with a final chapter on implementing the research into the curriculum.

Marzano, Robert J., Debra J. Pickering, and Jane E. Pollock. *Classroom Instruction that Works: Research-Based Strategies for Increasing Student Achievement.* ASCD, 2001. A part of the "What Works Series," selected well-researched strategies are presented, described, and defended.

Road to 21st Century Learning: a Policymakers' Guide to 21st Century Skills, The. Partnership for 21st Century Skills, 2004. A handbook for government officers, boards, and other policy-making bodies concerning the place of technology in education. See: www.21stcenturyskills.org

Silver, Harvey F., Richard W. Strong, and Matthew J. Perini. *So Each May Learn: Integrating Learning Syles and Multiple Intelligences*. ASCD, 2000. A practical guide to the ideas of Howard Gardner with good examples for integrating and assessing the Gardner strategies.

Strong, Richard W., Harvey F. Silver, and Mathew J. Perini. *Teaching What Matter's Most: Standards and Strategies for Raising Student Achievement*. ASCD, 2001. We are impressed with the idea that good teaching requires raised expectations, particularly when students are working in information-rich environments.

Wiggins & McTigue. *Understanding By Design*. ASCD, 1999. A classic in the field of education and the foundation work for the Understanding by Design movement in education.

Wiggins & McTigue. *Understanding By Design Handbook*. ASCD, 2004. Even better than the original, this treasury of ideas, forms, suggestions, and helps brings the entire Understanding by Design concept into practical application.

Brief Mention

Armstrong, Tricia. *Information Transformation: Teaching strategies for authentic research, projects, and activities*. Markham, ON: Pembroke Publishers, 2000.

Bromely, Karen. *Graphic Organizers: Visual Strategies for Active Learning*. Toronto, ON: Scholastic, 1995.

Daniels, Harvey. *Literature Circles*. York, ME: Stenhouse, 1994.

Galbraith, McClelland. et Al. *Analyzing Issues: Science, Technology & Society*. Toronto, ON: Trifolium Books, 1996.

Harvey, Stephanie and Goudvis. *Strategies That Work*. York, ME: Stenhouse Publishers, 2000.

Harvey, Stephanie. *Nonfiction Matters: Reading, Writing, and Research in Grades 3–8.*York Me: Stenhouse Publishers, 1998.

Hyerle, David. *Visual Tools for Constructing Knowledge*. Alexandria, VA: Association for Supervision and Curriculum Development, 1996.

Koechlin, Carol and Sandi Zwaan. *Information Power Pack Intermediate Skillsbook*. Markham, ON. Pembroke, 1997.

Koechlin, Carol and Sandi Zwaan. *Information Power Pack Junior Skillsbook.* Markham, ON. Pembroke, 1997,

Koechlin, Carol and Sandi Zwaan. *Teaching Tools for the Information Age.* Markham, ON. Pembroke, 1997.

Lundy, Kathleen Gould. *What do I do about the kid who...?: 50 ways to turn teaching into learning.* Toronto: Pembroke Publishers, 2004.

Moline, Steve. *I See What you Mean: Children at Work With Visual Information K–8.* York, ME : Stenhouse, 1995.

Morgan, Nora and Juliana Saxton. *Asking Better Questions: Models, Techniques and Classroom Activities for Engaging Students in Learning.* Markham, ON: Pembroke, 1994.

Parry, Terence and Gayle Gregory. *Designing Brain Compatible Learning.* Arlington Heights: Skylight, 1998.

Wolfe, Patricia. *Brain Matters: Translating Research into Classroom Practice.* Alexandria VA: Association Supervision and Curriculum Development, 2001.

Websites

From Now On: The Educational Technology Journal, by Jamie McKenzie
http://www.fno.org

The Graphic Organizer
www.graphic.org/

Jigsaw Classroom
http://www.jigsaw.org/

The WebQuest Page
http://edweb.sdsu.edu/webquest/webquest.html

Index